THE LISTOWEL LITERARY
PHENOMENON

THE LISTOWEL LITERARY PHENOMENON

North Kerry Writers – A Critical Introduction

Edited by
Gabriel Fitzmaurice

Cló Iar-Chonnachta
Indreabhán
Conamara

First published in 1994 by
Cló Iar-Chonnachta Teo.

© Respective Authors 1994

ISBN 1 874700 87 7

Cover Artwork:
Brian Bourke

Cover Design:
Johan Hofsteenge

Design:
C.I.C.

Cló Iar-Chonnachta receives financial assistance from the
Arts Council/An Chomhairle Ealaíon

Publisher: Cló Iar-Chonnachta Teo, Indreabhán, Conamara.
    Tel: 091-93307   Fax: 091-93362
Printing: Clódóirí Lurgan Teo., Indreabhán, Conamara.
    Tel: 091-93251/93157

George Fitzmaurice (1877 – 1963)

Maurice Walsh (1879 – 1964)

Thomas MacGreevy (1893 – 1967)

Bryan MacMahon (1909 –   )

John B. Keane (1928 –   )

Brendan Kennelly (1936 –   )

Gabriel Fitzmaurice (1952 –   )

CONTENTS

INTRODUCTION

This book is the result of a series of lectures I commissioned (between 1987 and 1992) at Writers' Week, Listowel, dealing with North Kerry writers and writing. It seemed appropriate to gather the lectures (or essays based on them) in book form.

The first thing that must be said is that not all the significant writers of North Kerry are collected here. This book deals with creative writers only – thus there is no space for essays on John Coolahan, Pádraig A. de Brún, J. Anthony Gaughan, Monsignor Edward J. Kissane, Mick McCarthy, F.X. Martin, Joesph O' Connor, the O'Rahillys (Alfred, Cecile and Thomas F.) *et al*. Nor has space been allotted to creative writers such as Maureen Beasley, Robert Leslie Boland, Paddy Drury, Willie 'the Poet' Finucane, Paddy Fitzgibbon, Patrick Given, Dan Keane, James A. Kelly, Patrick Kennelly, Seán McCarthy, Seamus Wilmot, and the rest. *Beidh lá eile ag na Paoraigh*!

The question that is frequently asked is how is it that the Listowel area has thrown up so many good writers? The answers are various – none of them, to my mind, entirely satisfactory. The common answers are that there is a traditional love of learning in the area; that there is a strong classical tradition in the area; that the area is an enclosed, gossipy one with a love of fine words, poetry, song and story; that the people of North Kerry are great talkers; that North Kerry inhabits an area fertilized by two languages (Irish and English). And so on. . . Certainly all these conditions exist in North Kerry. Or they did up to recently. But the same could be said of many areas. It's a phenomenon I don't understand. Is it just a monumental fluke, or is there something else at work? I honestly don't know. I can only talk from my experience.

Moyvane, the village where I grew up, and still live in, seven miles from Listowel, was full of songs and stories. There was no television when I was growing up (I was born in 1952) and very few radios. Very few people read books, but the oral tradition was strong. There was no *seanchaí* in the village, but there were stories and songs, snatches of sporting derring–do, ghost stories to scare us children into staying home at night, stories of *piseogs*, snippets of local history, the lore of neighbours 'rambling' to each others houses – the first question always asked was "Any news?". . . We lived in a strange world half-way between the empirical world of the rational mind and the magical world of superstition. Some of the ghost stories we were told were believed as much by their tellers as by ourselves.

Things 'ran in families': The Cunninghams, my mother's people, 'had brains'. My grandfather, Maurice Cunningham, was a poet. I wasn't aware of that until 1984 when I stumbled across it in a very strange way. My distant cousin, Mary Anne Cunningham (Mrs. Ned Liston of Athea, a neighbouring village), a woman of advancing years, called me aside shortly after *Rainsong*, my first collection, was published that Summer. She congratulated me on its publication and confided in me that she was glad I was writing poetry. I took it simply as a compliment until she revealed her real reason for congratulating me. After my grandfather died, she, alone among the Cunninghams, took up the poet's pen. The *piseog* ran that when the poetry passed to the distaff side of the family, the poetry died out of that family in that generation. I was the next generation. The poetry had passed on.

I remember, too, as a young boy the talk about a new play, *Sive*, in 1960 or thereabouts. Cars were hired to take the 'literati' of the village to Listowel where *Sive* was playing. My father and mother hired a car to take them to see it too. The village was agog with this new play. Stories began to filter through about its author, John B. Keane: He stayed up all night writing . . . He read books while eating . . . To my impressionable mind, that was high romance, far away from the reality of surviving in a small village. I wanted that too. I wanted people to be talking about me like that. I would have been about seven at the time!

And people used to come into our house to talk about literature. My mother had a passion for art – books, paintings, music – and spent much of her time reading when she became invalided. That was before her sight failed. Nonplussed, she borrowed 'talking books' from the Society for the Blind and encouraged me to listen to her favourite classics. I remember, too, a local Parish Priest who used consult her. He would occassionally present her with a 'doubtful' book (where he got them, I'll never know) for her opinion. That's how I first read *The Country Girls*! My mother gave it to me. And the poor penitent who had confessed to reading it never knew! My mother had the greatest influence upon me. I wouldn't have become a writer without her. I deeply regret that she didn't live to see, apart from juvenilia in college magazines, a single line of mine in print.

In North Kerry there's something to live up to, something to pit yourself against, if you're a writer. There's little doubt in my mind that a writing tradition creates writers – as a footballing tradition creates footballers and so on. And there's an audience too. An audience for song and story, poetry and plays. Anywhere there's fine talk, the people of North Kerry will flock to hear it – and put in their own 'spake' too!

Of course, there's no accounting for genius. It's a matter of awe that the Listowel area has, for well over a hundred years now, regularly produced worthwhile writers, some of them writers of genius. It remains a mystery, and like all mysteries, defies explanation. All we can do is wonder about it. In wonder writing begins . . .

The essays collected here mark a beginning – the first published, systematic attempt to come to terms with 'the Listowel phenomenon'. Each of the contributors braved the gauntlet of the Listowel audience at various Writers' Weeks. They were listened to with interest and delight for they bore good news. They came to praise 'the Listowel writers', not to bury them. They were honest in their celebration, but one cannot help wondering what was left unsaid. In welcoming this volume, I await its *alter ego* – the adverse critique every writer anticipates with curiosity and fear.

Gabriel Fitzmaurice
Moyvane, Co. Kerry.

THE MAGIC GLASSES OF GEORGE FITZMAURICE
BY FINTAN O'TOOLE

In India a thousand years ago, they said that demons tried to break up the first performance of the first play. The demons did this because they believed that by including themselves on the same level as mere humans, the drama shamed them. The God Brahma appeared and made a speech to the unruly demons:

"In drama there is no exclusive representation of you demons or of the gods. Drama is a representation of the emotional states of the threefold universe. It includes concerns of duty, play, material gain, peace, mirth, war, desire and death. It teaches duty to those who violate duty, desire to those addicted to love; it reprimands those who behave rudely, promotes restraint in those who are disciplined; it gives courage to cowards, energy to heroes; it enlightens fools and gives learning to learned men."[1]

So saying, Brahma ordered that a playhouse be built to protect the drama from the demons. This myth of origin, rather than a long account of the beginnings of the Irish Literary Theatre, seems to me to be a more appropriate beginning for a discussion of the plays of George Fitzmaurice. In his work, and the work of his North Kerry successors, there is a playwright who does not believe that anyone is shamed when gods and demons – the forces of the supernatural world – are included on the same level as human beings. There is Brahma's belief, expressed in a Swiftian satire, that the theatre can teach us things about how to live, enlightening fools and giving learning to learned men. There are the great concerns of duty, play, money, peace, mirth, war, desire and death. There is the sense of a kind of theatre that has to be housed within the walls of a playhouse in order to be protected but that has its origins in

---

[1] *Theatre of Memory: The Plays of Kalidasa*, edited by Barbara Stroller Miller, Columbia University Press, New York, 1984. p. 15

the days before there were theatre buildings. And, above all, in Fitzmaurice's theatre, there are the demons just outside the door, banging on the walls, threatening to invade the stage angry, unpredictable and troublesome. For Fitzmaurice brought those dark forces of the cosmos, the wild and malicious demons, back into contemporary writing, in a way that harks back to those Indian dramas, or forward to the theatre of contemporary Africa. The great lost soul of modern Irish theatre, he could never really fit the world-view of the Revival and became its most shameful victim. Yet the time has come to recognise him as one of the great 20th century Irish playwrights, and indeed as a figure of international significance.

What I want to suggest is that in the world of 20th century literature, the phrase the Kingdom of Kerry is more than just a parochial conceit. The case that what has gone on in North Kerry writing is something quite separate from and needs to be understood differently to, the rest of Irish writing, is at least an arguable one. The awkward status within the canon of George Fitzmaurice, John B. Keane and Bryan MacMahon offers at least prima facie evidence. (MacMahon and Fitzmaurice, for instance don't appear in The Field Day Anthology of Irish Writing. Keane is represented by a brief extract.) Fitzmaurice's actual expulsion from the league of great Abbey dramatists in spite of being one of the theatre's earliest and finest writers, is a more direct pointer. What is more, this marginalisation has logic to it. There is a separate discourse conducted by the North Kerry writers, and Fitzmaurice in particular, to the one which operated within the Irish Literary Revival. The work of Fitzmaurice cannot be properly understood if it is approached from the point of view of the movement that spawned Yeats and Synge and O'Casey. His Kingdom is not of their world. And in suggesting this, I am not attempting to narrow the range of his writing, to reduce it to the status of a petty, local little thing of no concern to anyone outside of the Kingdom, but to suggest the opposite: that if we want to seek points of contact with this work, we have to look beyond Dublin, to Lorca, to the writers of Latin America, to a writer like the Nigerian poet and playwright

Wole Soyinka. Fitzmaurice discovered his own kind of magic realism, long before the term came to be applied to writers like Gabriel Garcia Marquez or Salman Rushdie.

The exclusion of Fitzmaurice from the Abbey Theatre is perhaps the most poignant and shameful story of that theatre's history. It is not that rejection by the Abbey was an unparalleled fate. What is unparalleled, though, is the failure of a writer of real stature to find an alternative home of some sort after rejection by the Abbey. Sean O'Casey had England and Broadway. Denis Johnston had the Gate and later the Abbey itself. Brendan Behan and Tom Murphy had Joan Littlewood's Theatre Royal, Stratford East. John B. Keane had first an amateur and then a commercial theatre to turn to. But, aside from the efforts of Austin Clarke and the Lyric, Fitzmaurice had no alternative home. His work was too strange when it was good, and too mediocre when it was not strange, to be easily taken up by anyone else. His last new play accepted by the Abbey was staged in 1923. When he died 40 years later, he left behind the most heart-rending literary legacy in Irish theatrical history, a single battered suitcase found beside his bed containing copies of his published plays and manuscripts of his many unpublished ones with a note in pencil attached to them: "Author is prepared to sell outright all rights in 14 plays dealing intimately with life in the Irish countryside. Most have already been either printed or published. Suitable to which to build musical, television etc. Pass to anyone interested."[1]

The sadness of that neglect for both Fitzmaurice himself and the Irish theatre is obvious enough. What is less obvious is why this great divergence between Fitzmaurice and the Irish theatre movement should have happened. In trying to answer this question, our approach to Fitzmaurice is complicated by the fact that while Fitzmaurice has in recent years been rescued from his enemies he is is still in need of being rescued from his friends. The re-establishment of

---

[1] See the introductions to the three volumes of Fitzmaurice plays published as *Dramatic Fantasies* (1967), *Folk Plays* (1970) and *Realistic Plays* (1970) by Dolmen Press, Dublin.

Fitzmaurice's reputation in the early 1970s (a venture only partially successful in that it has yet to be fully validated in the only place where his reputation can really live – the theatre) was achieved by stressing his authenticity as a folk writer. Too much, in general, was taken on face value, too little made of the humour, the sophistication, the downright mischief of Fitzmaurice's writing.

The oddity of his achievement, the fact that his best work lies in the short plays of the supernatural and the natural which defy categorisation, was treated as a source of embarrassment rather than a cause for celebration. In the argument for Fitzmaurice as a folk writer, the tendency of his work to send up everything from folk tradition to the Catholic church to William Butler Yeats was missed. What we need to do now is to understand first of all that Fitzmaurice's great predecessor is not a *seanchaí* sitting by a fire, but another Irish Protestant who brought reality and fantasy into sharp and violent contact in order to disrupt both: Johnathan Swift. Fitzmaurice's kingdom is not a million miles from Lilliput or Brobdingnag.

To begin to understand Fitzmaurice, and to understand his expulsion from the Abbey by the Archangel Yeats, we have to begin with a fundamental difference between his attitude of mind and that of the revivalists. It is not just that they went to the theatre while he went to the music halls, that they campaigned against conscription while he joined up and served in the trenches, that they were Protestants in search of an accomodation with Catholic Ireland, while he was born, as the child of Protestant and Catholic parents, into precisely such an accomodation, though these things are far from irrelevant. They point to the fact that Fitzmaurice accepted the world while they went about inventing a world, that he was at home in the 20th century while they felt themselves to be, in some degree, refugees from it. What is crucial is the manifestation of these differences in the respective attitudes to the world of folklore of Yeats and Lady Gregory on the one side and of Fitzmaurice on the other.

The revivalists' attitudes are summed up in the very word "revival". Something which has barely survived the onslaught of the modern world, some surviving relic of a fuller and more whole civilisation is to be brought back to life. And this revival works in another way, too. It is also a part of a national revival, the coming back to life of a half-dead nation. It is at once an act of homage to an imagined past and an act of present-day political resurrection.

In *The Celtic Twilight* (1893) and after, Yeats went to the countryside and to folklore in search of a way of transcending modern urban materialism. He saw folklore as pure and primal, as a survival from a more unified culture, that of the middle ages. In his Nobel Prize acceptance address, for instance, Yeats said that the imagination and speech of modern Irish drama were founded upon a mediaeval poetic and he commented that he could track any modern folk expression back to classical times.[1]

In this, though he was probably repeating what he had heard from William Morris, he was being very much the 19th century colonial, except in his own country and among his own people. Nineteenth century theory, like nineteenth century colonial politics, saw foreign, "primitive" societies as relics of man's social beginnings, folk arts as relics of prehistoric spirtuality. By treating folklore as a relic, albeit a relic of a romantically-conceived, more wonderful and whole society, Yeats fell into this pattern. Yet he also distrusted the demonic and ferocious (indeed the Catholic) aspects of that folklore, and for a man who thought he was dealing with a sacred survivial, was not above using it for particular political purposes.

When Fitzmaurice came to use folklore in his theatre, he left the demons in. Yeats, literally, took them out. We can see this very directly in the case of Yeats' early play *The Countess Cathleen* (1889). Yeats took the story of the play from a folk-tale he had collected in *Fairy and Folk Tales of the Irish Peasantry* (1888) as *The Countess Kathleen O'Shea*. Though Yeats did not know it at first, the story, far from being a pure survival from the Irish middle-ages, was in fact an import from France, but that is neither, for the

---

[1] See William Butler Yeats, *Autobiographies* p. 386 and *Essays and Introductions* p. 517 (London, Macmillan).

moment, here nor there. In the original story, there are demons. Yeats, though, transforms these demons for political reasons into Englishmen, strangers with good manners who operate on free trade principles.[1]

Fitzmaurice, on the other hand, uses folklore not as a survival from some other age, but as part of modern life, not as an escape from the sordid material world but as a troublesome and inescapable part of it. He does not see it as a symbol of paradise lost, nor does he transform it into a symbol of contemporary political hatreds. He simply doesn't see it as symbolic at all. In his great plays of the supernatural and the natural, what is immediately striking is the acceptance of the demons and spirits, the world of folk belief, as being as real or unreal as the quotidian world. Just as Swift's giants and pygmies and talking horses and flying islands are described in *Gulliver's Travels* in the rational language of scientific exploration, so in Fitzmaurice's best plays what is most remarkable about the supernatural is the fact it is not remarkable at all.

Fitzmaurice's approach to folk material is at once more complex and more direct than Yeats'. Yeats took the language and the sense of the other-worldly. Fitzmaurice went to the core and took the form. And the important point is that is is the form of folk art which connects it to 20th century modernism rather to the Romanticism to which Yeats harked back. Concentration in time and place, emotional intensity, rapid action and minimal characterisation are as crucial to folk ballads or mumming plays as they are to 20th century expressionistic art and theatre. The important Fitzmaurice, the Fitzmaurice of the short one-act plays usually called "Dramatic Fantasies", found in folklore a form which placed him, not with the revivers of a peasant culture, but with the avant garde of European modernism.

Only the obsession with a national literature, with the idea of Irish writing as a revival continuous with the Irish

---

[1] For a discussion of Yeats' use of folklore in *The Countess Cathleen* see Adrian Frazier, *Behind the Scenes*, University of California Press, 1990, pp14-17.

past, could have prevented us from seeing the obvious connection between Fitzmaurice and the European avant garde of his time. For what Fitzmaurice was doing was by no means unique to North Kerry or to Ireland. It was of a piece with James Joyce or Pablo Picasso or Wassily Kandinsky, or even the American architect Frank Lloyd Wright. It is Joyce using traditional stories and songs; it is Lloyd Wright founding his modern architecture on the perception that "the true basis for any serious study of the art of architecture still lies in those indigenous structures, more humble buildings everywhere being to architecture what folklore is to literature, or folk-song is to music."[1] It is Kandinsky and Picasso taking their inspiration from peasant painting or the African maker of masks. Fitzmaurice is connected as a dramatist to Antoin Artaud looking to the folk art of Bali for a theatre not unlike Fitzmaurice's own: a theatre built not on dialogue which explores psychology and motivation, but a theatre that would unfold in movement and poetry, humour and startling violence, a theatre of delight and vague, profound terror. He is connected to Brecht's scrutiny of Chinese theatre for strange, alienating forms of theatre which would break the Aristotelian mould.

And naturally, but most ironically he is connected to Yeats, who came to want that sort of drama too but sought it in the Japanese Noh tradition rather than in the Irish folk drama that he seems hardly to have been aware of at all. We don't know whether or not Fitzmaurice knew Irish folk plays, but it is striking that he is the dramatist whose absence Henry Glassie lamented in *All Silver and No Brass*, an heir to the mummers:

"The mummers' play was perhaps too close. But it could have provided modern dramatists with guidance like that Kadinsky found in peasant painting, for it was spectacle of the kind they imagined: manneristic, poetic, strange. Captain Mummer tells us his play is not from the tradition of classical Western drama: 'The like of this was never acted

---

[1] *All Silver and No Brass: An Irish Christmas Mumming*, Henry Glassie, Brandon Books, 1983, p. 66

19

on a stage.' . . . With *Finnegans Wake* it pitches mythically between dream and awareness. Mumming is not a theoretical symbolic art like a medieval morality, nor is it empirical descriptive art like a play by Ibsen. It rises between those poles of western thought, falsifying their purity, uniting them in mysterious imagery."[1] This could be an exact description of Fitzmaurice's so-called fantasies, making him, at least in spirit, the successor to the mummers. For Fitzmaurice not only rises between the abstract and empirical poles of western thought, he dramatically subverts both of them, clearing a space for himself in which he can overturn all opposites.

Fitzmaurice is a great bamboozler of absolute oppositions. It seems neither irrelevant nor inconsequential that he is the Protesant son of a Catholic mother and one of the most genuinely Irish of Irish writers who goes off and joins the British Army. For in his work he is the destroyer of all such oppositions as Catholic and Protestant, Irish and British, Christian and Pagan, male and female, natural and supernatural. And if you bear in mind that he wrote at a time when the nationalist distinction between Irish and British was being established as a political fact, as the central feature of Irish culture, then it is not really suprising that he should have been expelled from that culture, cast out into the exterior darkness of "Author is prepared to sell outright all rights in 14 plays dealing intimately with life in the Irish countryside." For Fitzmaurice, in demolishing oppositions and undermining absolutes, is a profoundly subversive figure for the culture in which he lived.

Fitzmaurice's primary act of cheek is the breathtaking somersault he turns in relation to the attitude of the Protestant writer to the world of native Irish folklore. For the dominant figures of his time, for Yeats and Lady Gregory, the world of the Gaelic peasant is the world of the Other. It is that out there which has to be assimilated, drawn on, dealt with. It is a symbol of unity and wholeness which lies outside of their

---

[1] *All Sliver and No Brass: An Irish Christmas Mumming*, Henry Glassie, Brandon Books, 1983, p. 66

own divided modern consciousness. It is that which is not Protestant.

What Fitzmaurice does is to make folklore Protestant. He makes it a symbol and an extension of the modern Protestant individualist consciousness. In *The Linnaun Shee*, or *The Dandy Dolls*, in *The Pie Dish* or *The Magic Glasses*, it is the man most in thrall to folkloric belief, to the world of magic and the supernatural – Jamesie Kennelly, Roger Carmody, Leum Donoghue, Jaymony Shanahan[1] – who is most Protestant in his insistence on the rights of individual conscience, on the personal relationship with the supernatural world which is the essence of the Protestant frame of mind.

What is particularly significant in these plays is that instead of being a harkening back to a world of social unity and cultural wholeness as it would be in Yeats or Lady Gregory, this relationship to the supernatural, pagan world is a source of social division. The visionaries cause conflict in the social world around them, upsetting, not re-enforcing the pattern of life. In this supreme act of cheek, Fitzmaurice disrupts at once the medieval and the modern, the Gaelic and the Protestant. He subverts both alternatives then on offer as versions of Ireland by effectively melting them into each other.

This notion of the folkloric world as a disrupter of distinctions, a disturbing confusion of opposites rather than a confirmer of an ancient unity of being is in keeping with the nature of folk belief itself in a way that Yeats and Lady Gregory are not. In studying folk tales, Tzvetan Todorov has suggested a distinction between the marvellous, the uncanny and the fantastic, and on his analysis it is clear that Fitzmaurice's short plays are properly called fantastic. For Todorov, the marvellous simply involves literature which presents the supernatural but does not try to explain it; the uncanny uses what seems to be the supernatural but turns

---

[1] All except *The Pie Dish* are in Vol. 1 of *The Plays of George Fitzmaurice*. *The Pie Dish* is in Vol. 2.

out to be explicable by natural means.[1] But the fantastic
suspends itself between the rational and the irrational, the
natural and the supernatural. As he puts it, "the limit
between the physical and the mental, between matter and
spirit, between word and thing, ceases to be impervious . . .
The physical world and the spiritual world interpenetrate;
their fundamental categories are modified as a result." This
kind of fantasy, Fitzmaurice's kind, "uses words to recreate
a vision of the world before it was divided up by words,"[2]
which is to say, the world of the very small child.
Fitzmaurice's own sense of his characters as naughty old
children is thus entirely appropriate. What we are dealing
with is not the world of the innocent child, the pre-lapsarian
world of innocence for which Yeats and Lady Gregory
hankered. It is the dangerous, contradictory, perverse world
of the old child in which the very categories by which we
understand reality, the basic oppositions by which we
comprehend things, are confused.

That this is directly in opposition to Yeats' vision is clear
from the way in which *The Linnaun Shee*, for instance, can
be read as a direct send-up of one of the key texts of the Irish
Revival: Yeat's own Cathleen Ni Houlihan. In Yeats's play,
an old woman representing Ireland entices a young man
away from his home to serve her cause and as she leaves she
turns again into a young woman with the walk of a queen.
The Linnaun Shee sends this story up without mercy. Both
the ugliness of the old woman and the beauty of her younger
self feature, but both are parodied in grotesque and
rhapsodic descriptions. And when Jamesie goes off, to
follow this illusion, to pursue this dream, the woman turns
out to be playing a trick on him that is not supernatural or
mystical but all too natural and human, a catty act of
revenge. Having enticed Jamesie out, she goes off with a
younger and handsomer man. Far from being godly,
magical and heavenly, the supernatural is just an extension

---

[1] See *The World of the Irish Wonder Tale*, Elliot B. Gose Jr.,
  Brandon Books, Dingle, 1985 pp 1905 ff
[2] Gose, op. cit, p. 107

of the human, in all its foolishness, wickedness and perversity. The idea of an other-worldy spirituality and by extension, through the parody of Yeats, the idea of Romantic Ireland, are undermined. Jamesie returns, not full of heavenly visions, but back to the workaday world of adding the ha'pence to the pence. What is striking about this tone in Fitzmaurice is that far from being a mere disavowal of the subterranean Celtic heritage of Ireland, it is probably closer to the real nature of that heritage than all the romanticisations of the revival ever were. From what we know of the Celtic gods, they sound more like Fitzmaurice's vengeful and perverse supernatural figures than aloof Olympian deities. Anne Ross remarks of them that they "frequently entered the worlds of men and played tricks upon those they chanced upon. They were not invincible." In effect they were not unlike the grotesque figures of modern satire: exaggerated human figures whose very scale makes every grain of wickedness and stupidity the more obvious and glaring. It is in this sense that Fitzmaurice's use of the supernatural overlaps strongly with his moral intentions as a social satirist.

In Fitzmaurice's short plays, just as surely as in Swift's *Gulliver's Travels*, the creatures from another world – the Lilliputians, or the Linnaun Shee, the Brobdingnagians or the Grey Men – are really versions of our own human failings blown up and made strange, so that we can see them better. Fitzmaurice's fairies are spiteful, arbitrary, mean and cruel. It is only their power that sets them off from us mortals. And sometimes the magical is barely set off from the mundane at all. In *The Magic Glasses*, for instance, the glasses in question, through which Jaymoney sees such wonders, may indeed be magical, but they are more likely to be a mass-produced toy, sold to gullible countrymen for a good price. The very uncertainty in the mind of the audience is itself powerfully satiric, humbling as it does our pride in being able to tell the difference between a miracle and a ragman's bauble.

In talking about Fitzmaurice's best plays as fantasies the danger is that this keen awareness of human behaviour and of social change, of the ordinary details of contemporary life, is not given its due. The crucial thing about Fitzmaurice as a bamboozler of opposites is that he has a keen eye for both fantasy *and* reality, that his plays are never whimsical precisely because of their innate and unblinking realism. It is worth remembering that while Synge had the Abbey scouring the country for genuine Aran Island pampooties for his actors to wear, Fitzmaurice had *his* actors in genuine modern elasticated shoes. It is worth remembering that it is Fitzmaurice who gives the Irish stage one of its very first returned Yanks, Pat Connor in *The Country Dressmaker*: "Guess I hired no side-car, could see no side-car, and just took a fancy for a tramp, like, over these rural fields hithermost. Left baggage at railway depot yonder. Turned right into Mullarkey's saloon. Why they didn't know what was a cocktail!"[1] And it is certainly worth remembering who the scorn of these plays is directed against: the priests and the quack doctors who are placed on the same level; the strong money-grabbing farmers who are everywhere in Fitzmaurice's world; the silly fantasy that Jaymony sees through the magic glasses of "driving the Saxon invader before us," the ludicrous aspects of parish pump politics with "Rourke's son of Meenscubawn" that "knocked the eye out of Timothy Mascal at the election between Hassett and Dayse in the town of Listowel!"

And in fact, far from being a backward-looking primitive, far from wanting to stop the clock and hold on to a dying world, Fitzmaurice's satire is also directed at those who think they can ignore time and change. The "wicked old children" of Fitzmaurice's plays – characters like Leum in *The Pie Dish* and Jamesie in *The Linnaun Shee* – are cursed precisely by their belief that time can be cheated, by their delusion that if you ignore time, time will ignore you. The movement of time, in Fitzmaurice's plays, is ignored at your peril, and this embrace of change makes him anything but a revivalist. His achievement instead was to create a world that was distinctively Irish but utterly devoid of static sentimentality, of local piety or of the adoration of the past.

---

[1] Vol. 3. p. 35

Unafraid to see the world as complex and contradictory, as perverse and wonderful in all its perversity, he was an increasingly uncomfortable figure for a society looking for simple definitions of itself. Now that we are coming to think of Ireland as wonderful for its complexity and contradiction, rather than for its simplicity and purity, we are perhaps, at long last ready to think of ourselves as contemporaries of George Fitzmaurice.

MAURICE WALSH: A CRITICAL APPRECIATION
BY STEVE MATHESON

Introduction

It is reasonable to look to a writer's last words for some definitive statement about the man and his craft, about what makes the man tick and what makes his writing worth reading. Maurice Walsh was writing stories and poetry for over sixty years and his final collection, *The Smart Fellow* appeared just after his death, in 1964. In one of the stories, *The Missing Meerschaum*, he concludes:

> "We cannot believe, but, sometimes, in talk, we allow that that strange place dreamt of or invented was a warmly interesting place, a place of salt and humour, a friendly place, a place worth trying for in the human way of good and as little evil as possible."[1]

For me that encapsulates the whole man and his work. There was no harm in him and much that was good. In all my own research into his life and writing I never found a sharp word or thought attaching to him and given the love of the sly crack or deep barb so common in humankind, that is quite a tribute.

In this one sentence there are some key words and phrases:

- that strange place dreamt of or invented
- warmly interesting
- a place of salt and humour
- a friendly place
- worth trying for in the human way of good
- as little evil as possible

---

[1] *The Smart Fellow*, p. 135 (Chambers, 1964)

By 1964 the world was turning to television rather than books, to the realism of the streets (and American ones at that) rather than the clean Irish and Scottish outdoors that Maurice Walsh pictured in his mind's eye and painted in words in his stories. The wide land of Moray and of south west Ireland were increasingly as places "dreamt of or invented" and those places and the characters who peopled them were rapidly going out of fashion. But fashions change and the wheel turns. In a world seemingly hell-bent on self pollution, "green" issues have assumed political as well as social force and it may be that today the values Walsh built into his books will bear fresh examination and find again the revelance and appreciation they had fifty years ago.

Maurice Walsh never claimed to be a great writer or even a novelist but described himself simply as a writer of books, or in that endearingly old fashioned word, of "yarns". He wrote stories of warmly interesting places and people, both full of salt and humour. He acknowledged evil in the world but strove for the human way of good. His heroes do the decent thing and even his villains are not wholly evil, with the possible exception of Sir William Cosby in *Blackcock's Feather*. He wrote of the land and the open air – "The Gael tholes ill with indoors while the sun is above ground"[1] – and about peoples and places, saints and scholars, tinkers and lords, heroes and blackguards. Robert Hogan[2] described his books as "entertainments" and Walsh himself would not have been offended by the term. Indeed, entertaining they all are but there are some, like *Blackcock's Feather* and the magnificent *And No Quarter* which are real gems and stand comparison with the very finest historical novels.

Background

But first let us look briefly at the influences which shaped the man and coloured his writing.

---

[1] *Blackcock's Feather*, p. 59. (Chambers, 1932)

[2] *Dictionary of Irish Writers*, Ed. R. Hogan. p. 72 (Greenwood Press, 1979)

The first and strongest influence was that of his father, John Walsh of Ballydonoghue, a very well educated and widely read farmer who passed on to his son his own love of literature and learning. John had a fine collection of the classics – Scott, Dickens, Thackeray – as well as detective stories and the works of Conan Doyle. The young Walsh used to read over his father's shoulder in the evening and in *While Rivers Run* he describes reading his first book in this way – Robert Buchanan's *Matt: A Tale of a Caravan*.[1]

From his earliest years he heard stories from his father. John Walsh was steeped in legend and folk tales which were for him not at all about "strange places dreamt or invented", but very much part of life. He passed on to his son a good deal of his own awareness of the uncanny in life as well as of the marvellous in literature. And it was from John Walsh of Ballydonoghue that Maurice Walsh got his first information of something that was to imbue his books, the theory of place as a force in shaping people and events.

"A place acquires an entity of its own, an entity that is the essence of all the life and thoughts and griefs and joys that have gone before."[2]

In almost all his books, the place where the action takes place is important in its own right. While the dialogue may sparkle, the characters may be drawn firmly and vividly and the action may be swift and exciting, behind all it is often the descriptions and the evocations of places that give his books their distinct richness. He writes with painter's eye but also with his father's deep understanding of the land itself. Whatever place he uses in his stories, the heroes take strength from it and the villains are weakened by their lack of ties to it or understanding of it.

"I want to contrast your young land with this old one that has been peopled for ten thousand years – or

---

[1] *While Rivers Run*, pp. 195/6 (Chambers, 1927)
[2] *Son of a Tinker*, p. 167 (Chambers, 1951)

thirty thousand. It has been closely peopled too, and has absorbed the mentality of many races. Man is no longer himself here. He belongs to the place. There is some subtle evocation – aura is better – some subtle aura of old times and old ways, old wisdoms – old wickednesses also – that affect and claim a man."[1]

It is fundamental to so many of his books – and perhaps the Scottish ones especially – that the history and experience of a place and the lingering influence of all that has gone on there before go to shape the people who live in that place and to speak to the people who pass through it, if they can hear. The two places dearest to Walsh's heart were his native Kerry and his adopted Scottish Highlands. They sang to him long after he was separated from them, vivid in his mind's eye, intense in his recollection and he peopled them with rich characters from experience and from imagination. Those characters and the places he set them in become congruent in the reader's imagination as in Walsh's own and the significance of the place itself is far beyond merely a convenient setting for the action. That understanding came from John Walsh and it was a great gift.

Another strong influence was his first teacher at Lisselton School, Michael Dillon, of whom it was said that if a child had any spark of learning in him, Michael would coax it out and help it grow.

Maurice Walsh had an uncomplicated childhood with the benefit of devoted parents and a large, happy family. He found much to occupy and satisfy him in Ballydonoghue and Listowel, was good with his hands and enjoyed lots of outdoor activities, swimming and shooting, boxing, football and fishing. But there was also a deeply imaginative side to him. It came out in his talent for drawing and in his appreciation for the sensibilities of people as well as the aura of places. He claimed to have seen ghosts on several

---

[1] *While Rivers Run*, p. 76.

occasions and thought nothing of it. Nor did John Walsh, of course.

So with that kind of sensitivity, and the benefit of his father's books and stories, it was not surprising that he began to write stories himself at an early age. His first publication was while he was still at school in the early 1890's, when he won a competition for a story in *The Weekly Freeman*. It was about bushranging in Australia and he said himself later that it came from reading Rolf Bolderwood's *Robbery under Arms*. As a boy he read avidly and was much taken with the works of Bulwer Lytton and "Monk" Lewis and the historical romances of G.P.R. James. It was George James's *Richelieu: A Tale of France* which inspired his own early historical efforts for the *Irish Emerald*. These early pieces are slight. Interesting to look back on but they give little hint of what was to come.

First he had a career to build. He entered the Civil Service, in the Excise, in 1901 and had an early move to Scotland where he was to spend most of the next twenty five years and acquire a Scottish wife, Caroline, the inspiration for the many red headed women in his books.

Maurice Walsh found huge satisfaction in the Excise Service and in Scotland. In the Excise Service, which he had entered mainly to please his mother, he found a tradition and a set of fellow officers which he admired.

> "A loosely shackled friendship of men . . . who will do their day's work efficiently, because work should be done efficiently, and thereafter be brothers to a prince or fellows to a beggar, if found worthy."[1]

In the Scottish Highlands, in the wide province of Moray, in Dufftown and Speyside he found a land and people he soon came to love. Both the Service and the land were to influence the young man strongly as he grew into experience and maturity. At the turn of the century he was an easy going but energetic young man, protected in the

---

[1] 1926 Council Report, Comhaltas Cana.

midst of a loving family and with little experience of the wider world. He was (and remained all his life) generous to a fault with his friends and the friends of his friends, gay and insatiably curious about people and places. But even then he was showing signs of resolution and determination and rigorous personal honesty. In widening his experience in Scotland during the first quarter of this century he developed further his personal code of integrity, staunchness and friendship which characterised his later life and which coloured the books he wrote. He had from his father an innate sense of the fitness of people and places and from his mother a strong moral sense of right and wrong. In the Excise Service of the time he found people with whom he could share strong principles and ideals as well as fierce discussion and the love of song and story. All were to shape the writer to come.

Output

Busy though he was with living, Walsh continued to think about writing and produced some work. In 1908 he had serialised in the *Irish Emerald* a story about the sack of Athenree. Nearly twenty five years later that story was to be transformed into *Blackcock's Feather*. The difference between the two, in style, imagination, characterisation and pace is considerable. The first is an interesting transitory piece, while the second has stood and will go on standing the test of time.

In the early 1920's he began producing stories for *The Dublin Magazine* but it was not until 1925 that *The Key Above the Door* appeared and set in chain the spate of books to follow. By that time Maurice had been back in Ireland for three years, having volunteered to return to join the Free State Excise Service.

Over the following 38 years Maurice Walsh produced another 19 books, a play and a variety of articles for magazines and papers. I shall deal here only with the books, which fall into five broad groups, with some overlap.

The Scottish stories
The Irish stories
Those with historical or folklore settings
The short story collections
The detective stories.

Those I have put into the Scottish category are:
The Key Above the Door (1926)
While Rivers Run (1928)
The Small Dark Man (1929)
The Hill Is Mine (1940)
The Spanish Lady (1943)
Trouble in the Glen (1950)

In the Irish category are:
The Road to Nowhere (1934)
Green Rushes (1935)
Castle Gillian (1948)
A Strange Woman's Daughter (1954)

The historical romances and folklore stories have Irish or Scottish settings (the place as a character in its own right again) but deserve a separate classification since they contain Walsh's finest work. They are:

Blackcock's Feather (1932)
And No Quarter (1937)
Sons of the Swordmaker (1938)
Son of Apple (1947)

The short stories too could be put into the Irish or Scottish categories but are more easily dealt with in a critical assessment as a group. The collections are:

Thomasheen James, Man-of-no-Work (1941)
Son of a Tinker (1951)
The Honest Fisherman (1954)
The Smart Fellow (1964)

The publication dates for these collections are a bit misleading since nearly all the stories appeared in magazines, particularly *The Saturday Evening Post*, before being gathered into collections.

In the final category there are two detective books:

The Man in Brown (1945)
Danger Under the Moon (1956)

though in truth "The Spanish Lady" could be described as his first detective story – and the best of them at that.

The Writer and his Times

Before we look at the works themselves in these five sometimes arbitrary categories I have suggested, it may be instructive to look at what influences were at work in writing (fiction, plays and poetry particularly) produced in Ireland in Walsh's time, at least between say the ending of the Civil War in 1923, Walsh's first entry into the published scene in 1926 and the outbreak of war in Europe in 1939/40.

A short (and very selective) chronology presents an interesting picture.

Year	Walsh	Other
1923	"The Woman without Mercy" (*Dublin Magazine*)	Civil War Ends Yeats receives Nobel Prize *Dublin Magazine* founded Seán O'Casey: *Shadow of a Gunman* Oliver St John Gogarty: *An Offering of Swans* F.R. Higgins: *The Salt Air* (poems) Elizabeth Bowen *Encounters*

		James Stephens: *Deirdre*
1924	"The Mission Sermon"	*Freeman's Journal* ceases
	(*Dublin Magazine*)	O'Casey: *Juno and the Paycock*
		Liam O'Flaherty: *Spring Sowing* *The Black Soul*
		T.C. Murray *Autumn Fire*
1925	"A Dialogue"	Yeats: *A Vision*
	(*Dublin Magazine*)	O'Flaherty: *The Informer*
		Edith Somerville *The Big House at Inver*
		F.R. Higgins: *Island Blood*
1926	*The Key Above the Door*	Raidio Éireann begins.
		Yeats: *Autobiographies* (6 vols.)
		O'Casey: *The Plough and the Stars*
		(Riots at the Abbey)
		O'Flaherty *Mr. Gilhooley*
		Seumas O'Sullivan: *Common Adventure*
1927		T.C. Murray: *The Pipe in the Fields*
		F.R. Higgins: *The Dark Breed*
		Conal O'Riordan: *Soldier Born*

1928	*While Rivers Run*	The Gate theatre opens
		T.C. Murray: *The Blind Wolf*
		O'Riordan: *Solider of Waterloo*
		O'Casey: *The Silver Tassie*
		Peadar O'Donnell: *Islanders*
		Yeats: *The Tower*
		Gogarty: *Wild Apples*
1929	*The Small Dark Man*	Censorship of Publication Act
		O'Flaherty: *The Mountain Tavern*
		Denis Johnston: *The Old Lady Says No*
1931		The Irish Press founded
		Frank O'Connor: *Guests of the Nation*
		Kate O'Brien: *Without My Cloak*
		Johnston: *The Moon in the Yellow River*
		Mary Manning: *Youth's the Season*
		Forrest Reid: *Uncle Stephen*
		L.A.G. Strong: *The Garden*
1932	*Blackcock's Feather*	Fianna Fáil government
		O'Connor:

The Saint and
Mary Kate
O'Flaherty:
Skerret
Sean O'Faolain:
Midsummer
Night's Madness
Padraic Colum:
Collected Poems
Austin Clarke:
The Bright
Temptation

1933   "The Quiet Man"   Strong: *Sea Wall*
(*Saturday Evening Post*)

1934   "The Road to Nowhere"   O'Faolain:
A Nest of Simple
Folk

Also   Yeats:
The Tower

"Then Came the Captain's   Patricia Lynch:
Daughter"   *The Turf*
(*Saturday Evening Post*)   *Cutter's Donkey*
Joesph O'Neill :
The Wind From the
North
Samuel Beckett:
More Pricks than
Kicks

1935   "Green Rushes"   Yeats:
Also   *A Full Moon in*
Mars

"Bad Town Dublin"   Bowen:
"Thirty Pieces of Copper"   *The House in*
Paris
(Both *Saturday Evening Post*)   Theresa Deevy: *The*
King of Spain's
Daughter

1936	"Prudent Dan"	Austin Clarke: *The Singing Men at Cashel*
	"Thomasheen James and the Canary Bird"	Francis MacManus: *Candle for the Proud*
	"Thomasheen James and the Running Dog" (All *Saturday Evening Post*)	O'Faolain: *Bird Alone* O'Connor: *Bones of Contention* P. Kavanagh *Ploughman*
1937	*And No Quarter*	Douglas Hyde becomes first President
	Also	T.C. Murray: *Spring Horizon*
	"Thomasheen James and the Absent Minded Professor"	Gogarty: *As I Was Going Down Sackville Street*
	"Thomasheen James and the Opprobius Name" (Both *Saturday Evening Post*)	O'Flaherty: *Famine* O'Connor: *The Big Fellow*
1938	"Sons of the Swordmaker"	Seumas McManus: *The Rocky Road to Dublin*
	Also	Kavanagh: *The Green Fool*
	"Thomasheen James and the Dangerous Age" (*Saturday Evening Post*)	Yeats: *Purgatory* Samuel Beckett: *Murphy* Bowen: *The Death of the Heart* Richard Hayward: *In Praise of Ulster*

| 1939 | "Thomasheen James and the Blind Pension" "Thomasheen James and the Birdlover" "Thomasheen James and the Deep Sea Pilot's Cap"

(All *Saturday Evening Post*) | World War II Ireland neutral Yeats dies.

James Joyce: *Finnegans Wake* Francis MacManus: *Men Withering* O'Casey: *I Knock at the Door* Paul Carroll: *The White Steed* Louis MacNiece: *Autumn Journal* Flann O'Brien: *At Swim Two Birds* |
|------|------|------|
| 1940 | *The Hill Is Mine*

Also | Start of The Bell. O'Casey: *Purple Dust* |

"Son of Apple" (Chambers Journal)
"Thomasheen James Jumps the Budget"
"Son of a Tinker"
  (Both *Saturday Evening Post*)
"Thomasheen James and the Gum Drop"
  (*Chicago Tribune*)
"Butcher to the Queen"
  (*The Bell*)
"Ireland in a Warring Europe"
  (*Saturday Evening Post*)

One could go on detailing the Walsh output against that of other writers through the forties and fifties but 1940 is a convenient place to stop for two reasons.

The first is the changing times themselves. The outbreak of war in Europe changed perceptions and expectations, in the United States as well as in Europe and fictional writing of the kind Maurice Walsh produced simply went out of fashion as reading tastes changed (or in face of competition from film and TV, simply disappeared). The break was not absolute of course and Walsh went on producing and selling books and stories for the next quarter of a century. But the decline really begins about 1940. There were compensations, though. Popularity in the United States, through the stories in the *Saturday Evening Post*, bought the attention of the film makers and "The Quiet Man" in particular had a huge success when the 1933 story was made into a film and released in 1952 after a world premiere in Ireland. Visualisation took the story to millions who would never have read it in text.

The second reason for halting this fairly arbitrary chronology of the Walsh canon against that of other writers is that by 1940 Walsh had produced his best work and there was little after 1940 to compare with what had been produced before. It is true that *The Spanish Lady* which came out in 1943 has very considerable merit but Walsh himself called it "the last squeeze of the bag"[1] and while he went on writing stories and articles competently, including his two detective stories, there are no truly memorable items to compare with, say, *And No Quarter* or *Blackcock's Feather*.

Assessment

It is possible and not too fanciful to find all sorts of echoes and influences in Walsh's work. Given that he, like his father before him, was immensely widely read, it would be surprising if such traces were not evident. But I can find no Irish influence which was decisive. If anything he owed more in the distant background to Stevenson and Scott than to Maria Edgeworth and Gerald Griffin. And probably more to the vivid memory of his father's folk tales and word spinning than to the long breathing spell of such seminal works as Douglas Hyde's "Love Songs of Connacht" though he took much delight in that work and in other folk works of a similar kind when they appeared. Who can say

---

[1] Letter to his niece, 21.11.44

how much he was influenced by the rich variety of offerings at the Abbey or the Gate, by the plays of Lennox Robinson or George Shiels? Articulate itinerants appear in lots of works. Walsh made use of the form but Jamesy Coffey is no one else's man than Maurice's own. Frank O'Connor's stories contain deep evocations of place that are critically important to the many plots and characters he found or devised in his long bicycle trips in search of Ireland and yet (to oversimplify too much), O'Connor's acute eye observes the place from without. Walsh, I think, senses and feels it more from within.

It was late in life before Walsh turned briefly to folklore tradition with works like *Sons of the Swordmaker* and *Son of Apple* but there are fragments of thought and language throughout the earlier works which pick up the sensitive awareness of the aura of past times and traditions which permeate such works as those of the Mayo poet Frederick Higgins who was writing in the twenties.

There is little in the Walsh work to reflect the dark visions of the plays of T.C. Murray whom Walsh knew when Murray was a headmaster at Inchicore while Walsh was working at the silent distillery there and yet there is an echo in Walsh's strangest book which had started as a play itself, *A Strange Woman's Daughter*.

Maurice Walsh also enjoyed the series of popular books written by Conal O'Riordan in the twenties and thirties, particularly the David Quinn stories which took a contemporary character through a variety of different situations. No similar development in Walsh's own work, one might say, yet early on he was reaching towards a continuing central character in Hugh Forbes, who appeared in *The Small Dark Man* and *Green Rushes* and in Paddy Joe Long in two of his other books. His friend and fellow Exciseman and novelist Neil Gunn advised him strongly[1] to find such a device instead of searching constantly for wholly new characters. Thomasheen James evolved from that – and

---

[1] Letter from Neil M. Gunn, 1937.

the lucrative *Saturday Evening Post* market for extreme "Irish" characters.

There ought, perhaps, to be some useful comparison with the stories of Liam O'Flaherty. Yet the man from Aran's stories of the wilderness and the outdoor life have a harsher perspective than anything in Walsh. O'Flaherty was said to have been much influenced in his novels by Dostoevsky but there is nothing of the Russian genres in Maurice Walsh's stories.

By 1940 Beckett and Flann O'Brien were experimenting with form as well as satirical substance in ways which were quite outside Walsh's experience or inclination. The world was moving on in a different direction.

Robert Hogan[1] has suggested three basic divisions in Irish writing this century:

– first the idealised portrayal based on rural culture and ancient history, looking back to Synge, Hyde and Moore and forward to the writers of the Irish Renaissance;
– second the formal experimentation in style and more critical content from Yeats and Joyce, leading on to O'Connor and O'Faoláin;
– third the present, which he sees as starting perhaps with writers like Austin Clarke and Flann O'Brien.

These are over simple distinctions but using them as a broad guide, where would Maurice Walsh fit in? Not in the third category, certainly, but not very easily into the other two either. He has some affinity with individual writers but little with movements. In his descriptions of the open air and the theory of place one could make a linkage with Lady Gregory and later with Padraic Colum and T.C. Murray and perhaps in the historical and folklore books with Joesph O'Neill but all these connections are faint and the right

---

[1] R. Hogan, ibid, pp 73/74

course seems to me to be to avoid trying to link him artificially with any particular Irish school or development.

Irish he certainly was and Ireland and the Irish in all their many manifestations were intensely important to him. He loved Scotland and the Scots but it was in Ireland that his deep roots lay. He was always careful to distinguish between the British people and their Empire – or "their bloody Empire" as he used to say – and was a fierce defender of the Irish heritage. Nowhere did he express that more eloquently than in his bold defence of Irish neutrality in the *Saturday Evening Post* in the 1940 article "Ireland in a Warring Europe". Let me quote you just a few lines:

"This little island of ours has seen Europe grow. We may well boast a little. We have helped Europe to emerge from barbarism to civilisation. When the British ran through their woods painted like American Indians, we Irish were making the most delicate, and today priceless, objects of art. We preserved the language and letters of Greece when the Dark Ages had fallen on Europe. The footmarks of Irish scholars all over Europe in those early centuries – from the fifth to the twelfth – are the signposts of emergent culture on the continent. Through the centuries we have nourished the flame of our own particular philosophy of life. And as we look about us today we ask ourselves whether that flame that we nourish on our modest hearths, in our little island home, may not have some quality of purity and perfection that all the furnaces of the dynasts can never produce . . . There is here, and many of you have seen it and enjoyed it, a gentle mode of life such as only great age, and innate culture, and high heart, and long experience can create in any land."[1]

---

[1] *Saturday Evening Post*, January 1940.

Powerful stuff and it created a great storm. Seán O'Faolain and Maurice Walsh had planned it together but it was pure Walsh speaking – and from the heart.

In the first quarter of the century Maurice Walsh was putting down his second set of roots, in Moray in Scotland, finding a wife and starting a family. He was writing very little and so stayed outside contemporary influences and pressures. When he began to write seriously, there was something wholesomely refreshing but also already a little old fashioned about his books. Names like Agnes de Burc and notions like taking an estate for the season without any commercial exploitation seem outdated and even antique today. The plots of the early books lack relevance by today's experience but they were always thin anyway and mere vehicles for descriptions of wide vistas of sun and sky, mountain and sea, against which interesting if not compelling characters bustle in and out of incident with verve and vigour.

Let us look at the five broad categories of Walsh's work in turn to see if we can bring out what gave his books their undoubted mass appeal at one time and how that appeal stands up to examination today.

The six books in the Scottish group all make pleasant reading still though all now have a distinctly old-fashioned air. Two (*The Small Dark Man* and *The Spanish Lady*) still have considerable grip and finely drawn characterisation while the others would sit less easily with modern tastes.

The first in the group was *The Key Above the Door* and it brought Maurice Walsh instant fame because of its unsolicited tribute from Sir James Barrie, who could instantly smell the heather in it. We know from Walsh's letters that it was written when he was lonely and on his own in Dublin, his wife and sons being in Scotland still. It was a deliberate attempt to recreate the atmosphere, sights and sense of the Highland scenes he loved and it succeeded well. He peopled the slight story with characters based very much on individuals he knew and set them in a lifestyle that was part his own and in part what he had seen and admired. The story is simple – the small Celtic hero eventually thrashes the big Southern bully and wins the woman – but it is told in a

43

straightforward, pleasant style interspersing philosophy (without pedantry), high humour and clean romance with fishing and shooting and deft development towards the inevitable savage fight at the end. But the great appeal was that the whole was set against the pure Highland scene, the freshness and vitality of which illuminate every chapter. The author has a painter's eye for a scene but each graphic description of mountain and loch comes from experience and the heart. It was a winning formula and it is easy to see why Barrie was so captivated by it.

The second book published, also in the Scottish group, was *While Rivers Run*. It has broadly the same Highland setting and some of the same characters in minor roles but it introduces an American and a sardonically humorous Irishman, Paddy Joe Long, who were to appear again in one of the Irish settings – *The Road to Nowhere*. There is little plot as such and no villain (but still a few fights) and this is a tale of a group of people working out their relationships with each other and, importantly, with the place they happen to be in. The book meets many of the criteria I set out at the beginning of this assessment – it is warmly interesting and friendly and has both salt and humour, especially in Paddy Joe Long. It has no evil in it. But in this book we see the deft storyteller honing his craft in a few tales within the wider tale which immediately whet the appetite for more of the same – like the story of the Kerry Blue terrier.

With the third book in the Scottish group – and the third book in sequence to be published – it is clear that the storyteller has found his metier and his power begins to move towards full maturity. "The Small Dark Man" relies again on a very simple structure but the characterisation has real depth and the atmosphere building is intense. It is a richly satisfying tale, swiftly but subtly told and enlivened both by experience and rich imagination.

The central character, Hugh Forbes, an Irishman come to Scotland, is a masterpiece, a small, resolute, quirky, steadfast, humorous individual with a cheerful but still deeply sensitive nature and a vast pride of race. His coming to Innismor in the Highlands of Scotland sets the glen awhirl. The book teems with incident and atmosphere, well

illustrated in the vivid description of the local Games at Glenmart and the contest between Hugh Forbes and his friend, the laird himself, at the big stone. The tension is built up cleverly as the two men, the big man and the small, draw out their reserves putt by putt to add inches to their previous throws. The climactic fight, too, is a mouth-drying affair. The whole book is an adventure, to read from start to finish at a gallop and then start again to savour slowly. A master storyteller had arrived.

He proved that beyond doubt or reservation with his fourth book, *Blackcock's Feather*, but I return to that in a different group.

The next Scottish one was *The Hill Is Mine*, published in 1940. It introduces another American, more fully drawn now from Walsh's own experience in the mid West of the United States. It is a pleasant gentle story of the old order being dispossessed but the old ways and loyalties clinging on faithfully. But it is not a memorable yarn. There is no villain and little action.

The fifth book in the Scottish group, *The Spanish Lady* appeared in 1943 and can be described as memorable by any standard. The descriptions of the Highland scene are as crisp and fresh as ever, but this is also one of his best books for inventive characterisation.

And that is one of the Walsh secrets. When he was at his best he produced characters to stay in the mind long after the plot they were set in had disappeared. Think of :

– Archie McGillivray in *The Key Above the Door*
– Paddy Joe Long in *While Rivers Run*
– Diego Usted, Big Ellen and Ann Mendoza in *The Spanish Lady*
– Jamesy Coffey in *The Road to Nowhere*
and many others.

In *The Spanish Lady*, Maurice Walsh cleverly catches the cadences of Spanish speech in his hero, Diego Usted from Paraguay (but with a mother from the Scottish Highlands) and Ann Mendoza-Harper, mysterious woman from the Basque country. Ann Mendoza is one of Walsh's most striking heroines. Usually his older women, the matriarchs, are more strongly drawn and his heroines lack depth (it is the heroes and those they fight who really count in the yarns) but as his storytelling grew in power, all his characters, including the women, grew more complex. With Ann Mendoza-Harper Walsh created a mature, vibrant woman of beauty and passion and one with the sharp intelligence and strength of personality to match the hero, Diego Usted.

The last book in the Scottish group appeared in 1950. *Trouble in the Glen* was a lighter book altogether, though it has some robustly interesting Scottish tinkers, a harder, more cynical breed than those he portrays in his Irish stories. It was made into an overblown, disastrous film, miscasting Orson Welles as a tartan-clad South American grandee. Sanin Cejador y Mengues in the book was at first an unbending hidalgo but one with wisdom and vision. Holywood has much to answer for.

The Scottish group of books represent much of his earliest published work and chart his growth in confidence and range. They contain a lot of the humour and warmth of the man himself and are, for the most part, superbly told stories with vivid atmosphere and imagery. They are all stories of the outdoors, the natural habitat of the Gael, of the hill and the glen, the river and the loch, and the choice of language and structure reflects that.

These books also contain much of the Walsh poetry, though I do not propose to examine his talents in that area here. Suffice it to say that Walsh himself loved poetry but would never have presumed to call himself a poet. He was one, though, as the verses in *The Small Dark Man* illustrate, not to mention those in *Blackcock's Feather*, to which we shall come later. Listen to Hugh Forbes, heart sore but brave.

> The dawn and dusk are the same,
> And wine it inspires me no longer.
> To play at, and fail at, the game
> And be blithe, I would need to be stronger
> Than Finn or Cuchulain or Conal.

But maybe next year or next life
The wine will have flavour and savour,
And beauty shall pierce like a knife,
And in war I would laugh at a favour
From Finn or Cuchulain and Conal.

And again a love I may find,
Like the dusk of the dawn and the gloaming,
To take me and break me and grind,
And set me again to the roaming
With Finn and Cuchulain and Conal.[1]

This is the storyteller weaving his spells in sonorous invocation of names and sense and rhythm.

But he had some amusing verse too, as in Paddy Joe Long's songs in *While Rivers Run*:

For Ale it has a pleasing bite
And Wine a soothing smooth,
And Usquebaugh a blinding light
That gleams on naked truth.
But ale and wine and Usquebaugh
Have lost their taste for me
Since she to whom I'm tied by law
Drinks my share of the three.[2]

The Irish "group" contains four books, although again this is an artificial distinction since the Irish category overlaps with some of the others. They are:

The Road to Nowhere	(1934)
Green Rushes	(1935)
Castle Gillian	(1948)
A Strange Woman's Daughter	(1954)

---

[1] *The Small Dark Man*, pp 133/4. (Chambers, 1929)
[2] *While Rivers Run*, p 195.

Of course the "Irish" factor, if one can call it that, was present in all his books – what else with one so committed to Ireland and steeped in its stories and its land? Walsh introduced an Irishman into his first book as a minor but important character, a more developed Irishman – and a Kerryman at that – (Paddy Joe Long) into his second and a thorough, full blooded, glorious Kerryman (Hugh Forbes) into his third. Up to that point he had introduced Irishmen into a Scottish setting but with the fourth book *Blackcock's Feather*, he brought a Scot to Ireland. That book qualifies as Irish by any definition but I have chosen to consider it in the historical category and we shall come to it, with delight, later. However in the first book in the Irish group I have defined, the fifth published, a Scot is brought to Ireland again.

Rogan Stuart, stricken and adrift, loses himself in Ireland in tinker's garb and finds himself again not least through the help of Jamsey Coffey and his tinker's tail and their own, particular standards and code of conduct. The scene is Kerry, painted with love, with descriptions of Listowel town and Ballydonoghue and reference to John Walsh himself. A gem of a book, with the full blooded mix of hero and villain, a strongly drawn heroine, a fast moving and compelling plot and lots of colourful incident, all told in a deft and flowing style. Several screenplays were written as the opportunity to make a film were recognised but unfortunately they came to nothing. As Maurice Walsh himself said, the part of Jamesy Coffey was tailor made for Barry Fitzgerald.

Here we see Walsh on the surest possibe ground. Kerry, high, wide and handsome is the perfect backdrop for the interaction of characters and cultures that he paints with real skill and understanding, moving the plot and the relationships along with a deft, confident touch. The key words and phrases we identified at the beginning of this assessment can be readily identified here. To recap, they were:

"that strange place dreamt of or invented"
"warmly interesting"

"a place of salt and humour"
"a friendly place"
"worth trying for in the human way of good"
"as little evil as possible".

The tinker world was familiar enough in its harsh reality to Walsh in real life, but he had also met and was friendly with some real characters of the road and it was those he distilled into Jamesy Coffey. The characters are presented in a "warmly interesting" way in places of "salt and humour" with reference to "as little evil as possible" (though evil and the reality of life are certainly not ignored.) Walsh was wholly averse to moralising in his books (or in life) and he chose instead to let contrasts speak for themselves. The contrast of the hills and open spaces to the crowded life of cities. The contrast of the conventional standards of society to those of the fraternity of the roads. And if he idealised the latter a bit, he kept within the bounds of credibility and made the contrasts tell. In this book, for example, in describing the tinkers' camps and the roadmen's pubs, where all the best stories and songs were to be heard, he brought in some outsiders, "warmly interesting" right enough, but with the code and standards of ordinary society. And he made them see things in a different light. Not better or worse but different. He showed, without labouring or even explicitly stating the point that there are to be found in such places (and everywhere, Walsh would have argued) people and ideas "worth trying for in the human way of good".

In 1935, the second book in the Irish group appeared. *Green Rushes* was a collection of five short stories, linked through Hugh Forbes, of *The Small Dark Man*, in earlier times when he led a Flying Column in the Black and Tan war. The title has its origin in the old love saying:

"I will lay green rushes under her feet that she may step softly."

Each story relates the romance of a different character in the group, though not Hugh Forbes' own. The stories are set mostly in Kerry in or after the Troubles and the best of them is certainly *The Quiet Man*. That is a deftly structured, beautifully developed story of the quiet, strong, sensitive man forced at last to show his true strength against the brute. It combines the best elements of the storyteller's art, an essential simplicity of style and plot with a sonorous, rich language. The build up of tension throughout the story, leading to the inevitable, terrific fight at the end, is superbly handled, in the tradition of epic with the wings of fate hovering over all throughout.

But it has to be said that there are some seeds of disquiet to be discerned in this collection of connected stories. They are not all of the same quality and they suffer from having appeared first in magazines and not having been conceived as a whole. *The Quiet Man* appeared in its first form in the *Saturday Evening Post* in 1933 and it was the first of his stories to be placed in an American magazine. Many others were to follow and they led Walsh into a classic dilemma, whether to write for himself or for his publishers. Up to that point he had written what he wanted to write in his own way and for his own satisfaction. It was fortunate that what he produced pleased his readers in Ireland and Scotland. And initially in the United States also. But the Post and his US publishers wanted "Irish" stories with "Irish" characters and that was not always (or only) what Walsh himself wanted. But the magazine market was very rewarding financially, more so indeed than the royalties from the books themselves, and as a full time writer from the middle thirties, he had a family to keep. It was not a problem at first in the height of his popularity and it was never a major obstacle in that he was a storyteller first and a seller of stories only second, but the pressure to supply the market that would pay did have an effect.

Walsh himself was also a sentimental man and sometimes twisted coincidence to ensure a happy ending. Moreover, the depth of his imagery was always vivid and sometimes too rich to sustain the plots he built on.

So within *Green Rushes* there are both good and bad examples of Walsh's work. As well as *The Quiet Man* there is *Then Came the Captain's Daughter*, which is not a particularly good story in itself but has within it a separate story which is superb. The tale of little Ellen Moloney is a fairy story of great poignancy and tenderness, a beautiful tale of a father back from the grave to love and protect his own, an affirmation that love is stronger than death and a perfect gem of the storyteller's art. But the rest of the stories are of much lesser quality and *The Red Girl* is as near to a clumsily written tale as Walsh ever told, illustrating that defect his friend and fellow writer Neil Gunn identified early, the clash between what the storyteller knows is right for his art and what the professional writer knows his magazine editors want.

The third book in the Irish group was published in 1948. *Castle Gillian* is not a memorable tale, though the characterisation is sharp and the action brisk. The trouble is that he had been there before too often. Most of the story was conceived when Walsh was trying unsuccessfully to turn *The Road to Nowhere* into a screenplay.

A Strange Woman's Daughter, published in 1954, was the last book in the Irish group. It was not a success, far too rigid in structure and reflecting its origins as a play. The wise mad woman wandering the roads is a good, if unoriginal, idea but it does not come off here.

It is the third group of books, the historical romances and folklore stories, which to my mind contain Maurice Walsh's greatest achievements as a storyteller, a writer and a poet and which bring his work out of the category of "entertainments" and into comparison with the heavyweights. The four books in this group are:

Blackcock's Feather	(1932)
And No Quarter	(1937)
Sons of the Swordmaker	(1938)
Son of Apple	(1947)

The first of these, *Blackcock's Feather*, is of course very familiar still as it continues to be used in Irish schools as a text book today, though regretfully with some deletions – the poetry in particular. The basic story first appeared in the *Irish Emerald* in 1908 and created something of a stir even then but in its later version it is quite stunning in pace, characterisation, plot and style.

Briefly, David Gordon from the Highlands of Scotland, no friend on his father's account of Elizabethan England, comes after the death of that father to visit his cousin (on his mother's side) at Dungiven in Ireland, well outside the Pale. He comes in a time of truce but finds action aplenty in no time at all. The story proceeds at a magnificent gallop. The hero finds experience in war and in love, makes both friends and enemies among the English and finds deep and abiding kinship among the Gaels. It is a story of hot action and high romance, with the dunt of battle and the clasp of true friendship as well as the light of love thick among its pages.

There are in fact only two short pieces of verse in the whole book but they are magnificent, apt in the extreme in their context, vivid in their impact. First when David Gordon's cousin Donal is planning to rescue and carry off his sweetheart, locked up by her father in far Galway, the old *seanchaí* touches his harpstrings to make the soul shiver and sings the heart-stopping throat-aching "Song of Bright Una":

> "Girl, now that my eyes
> Again shall look long on you,
> Girl, now that my heart
> Is athirst in the drouth for you,
> Girl, now that my soul
> Yearns deep for the deeps in you,
> Now, while my life has a wing,
> Do I sing my song to you."[1]

There is more, which I will not repeat here. Read the book again!

Later in the book, a different mood calls for a different verse. David Gordon and a handful of men are trapped inside the walled and fortified town of Sligo after a fierce night of fighting and driving the Sasanach to and inside the

---

[1] *Blackcock's Feather*, pp 105/6.

gates. Throughout the night, in a welter and haze of blows, charge and counter charge, David Gordon had kept a cool head, marshalling his small troop of horses with care. But in the face of what looks like certain death at the end he throws off restraint and lets the swordsman in him have free rein, with the long, wicked, flickering blade of his Andrea Ferrara creating a legend of terror. And he sings as he fights, sings gaily and with pleasure "The Sword Song of Gillian the Black":

"I am the Sword – hammered and wrought
By Gillian, for Gillian.
Where now the swank men, lean men who fought
By Gillian, for Gillian?
Dust in the wind, clay in the rain,
Like Gillian, ho Gillian!
Still am I clean, blade without stain –
Dead Gillian, dust Gillian!"[1]

The whole book teems with incident but what makes it so outstanding is the ease of transition from fierce action to easy calm, from battle and riot to romance, from sharp dialogue to convivial conversation. The characterisation is excellent, from the hero himself, David Gordon (and the book is full of heroes, English and Irish as well as the Scot) to the nastiest and most brutal villain Walsh produced, Captain Sir William Cosby of Cong. From the earliest pages it is obvious that hero and villain are to fight to the death at the end and we are not disappointed. Fighting there is in plenty but much more. The easy companionship of men in the northern dun is deftly pictured, the deep and immediate friendship-binding kinship between David Gordon and his cousin, Donal, is a fine warming one and it is vividly painted from the moment of first meeting. And the tie between David Gordon and the old, gentle, fighting priest, Father Senan, is quite beautiful.

---

[1] *Blackcock's Feather*, p 265.

If *Blackcock's Feather* had been the only book Maurice wrote, he could stand on it secure that his reputation as a writer of stature would endure. Yet the next book in this group, *And No Quarter*, which appeared five years later, in 1937, is even better. Those five extra years of experience in his craft are put to good effect. The canvas is a big one since the story is set against the campaign waged by Montrose against the forces of the Covenant across the Highlands of Scotland in the middle 1600s. Martin Somers, surgeon and adjutant of women in O'Cahan's Irish regiment in the army of Montrose starts us with the battle of Tippermuir, takes us through the sack of Aberdeen and the bloody haze of Kilsyth to the rout at Philliphaugh and involves us in a multitude of incidents besides. There are two strong women, fair and dark: Margaret Anderson of the salty tongue and fierce independence, rescued from the stocks of the kirk in Aberdeen, and Isabel Rose, rescued from Ardclach where her father held her behind locked doors, and rescued again before the story ends. Both women's lifes are entwined with that of Martin Somers whether he likes it or not, in a love story which moves along now slowly, now swiftly against the clash of armies and the lightning forays of Montrose's Irish and Highland guerillas.

The discipline of the writing is quite striking. Walsh was ever inclined to over exuberance in his descriptions, his painter's eye impatient with his writer's limations in presenting the full vividness of scene or setting, but the control in this book is perfect. Walsh himself thought it his best effort and so too did his friend Neil Gunn, himself an austerely disciplined writer not given to praise for the sake of friendship only. In a letter to Walsh after first reading the manuscript, Gunn said:

> "I read it all in one long, dithering wallop . . .
> Tippermuir got me where I thought there was
> nothing of me left and it moved me, by God, like
> the war pipes.
> Cheers to you, boy! The atmosphere of that Gaelic
> camp is thick with easy life. And if you give the
> Covenant folk hell, they deserved most of it."

Praise indeed from a writer of very considerable stature in his own right. He gave Walsh some very pertinent advice about resisting suggestions from his publisher that some scenes, like the one taking Meg Anderson from the stocks outside the kirk, should be removed. And he put his finger on the balance Walsh achieved in his book.

"Your movement of masses, of armies, is good. The whole historic treatment is excellent and I can see your whole self shaping up every now and then to assessment and judgement – a thing that is new to you but which you carry of nobly.[1]"

Throughout the book, the writing has a sureness of touch that shows the true craftsman and a consciousness of style that manages to strike the right note in each succeeding passage. When Meg Anderson and some of the women of the camp are butchered by Balcarres' horse, the grief of the clans is too great to bear and I defy anyone to read without a tremor the throat catching passage that describes the return to camp and the burial. This is only a fragment:

"We buried our dead in the clear pale dawn and all the pipers marched behind playing the heart-aching "Soiridh: Farewell my Fair One". In Spynie Tower I had promised Margaret that parting tune, and she had it now, though her ears were deaf. And three Irish regiments and ten Highland clans marched behind her; she was wearing her silken gown but it did not swing, and her silver buckled shoon were on her feet; but she rode on no white horse and she had no silver girdle on the span of her waist.
Kilsyth was the vengeance Montrose led us to."[2]

---

[1] Letter from Neil Gunn, 23.2.37.
[2] *And No Quarter*, pp 262/3. (Chambers, 1937.)

The book is full of incident, and of course, of salt and humour, as well as sharply drawn, warmly interesting characters, like Martin Somer's foster brother, Tadhg Mor and the fleering, valiant Ranald Ban McKinnon of Mull.

Walsh was once considerably embarassed by Sean O Faolain comparing his talent to that of Robert Louis Stevenson but this is the book that justifies that. It stands comparison in scope and execution with Scott as well as Stevenson. It will have a timeless appeal.

Sons of the Swordmaker, which was published in the following year, 1938, is a quite different book, a bold attempt to recreate an ethos of a different age in the spirit of the sagas. It is very enjoyable but does not quite come off. Walsh had been experimenting with the form for some time. One version of the stories appeared in the *Dublin Magazine* as early as 1923, heavily imbued with the Celtic twilight. The later version in connected stories is more tightly written, as one would expect from someone of Walsh's experience and power by this time, but building a coherent whole in spirit and outlook was hard to achieve. In some ways, it was ahead of its time and did not fit easily into classification as historical romance or conventional novel or saga translated. But is is very well executed and the work of a confident craftsman.

The last book in the group, *Son of Apple* was written during the war years but not published until 1947. It does work. It is a rendering of an old folk tale translated from the Irish by Catriona Macleod but then given fresh life, vividness and humour by Walsh the master storyteller. It is a delightful fairy story of wizards, giants, magic and romance told in a light, simple style but with rich and yet delicate descriptive power. Walsh demonstrated here just how well he had learned to use his painter's eye and storyteller's gift to maximum effect.

In fact all four books in this category show Walsh the storyteller at the peak of his achievement. As historical romances or folklore rewoven, it is hard to see how they could be bettered.

The short story collections are gathered in four books:

Thomasheen James, Man-of-no-Work	(1941)
Son of a Tinker	(1951)
The Honest Fisherman	(1954)
The Smart Fellow	(1964)

Nearly all of these stories appeared in magazines before being collected and published in book form. *Thomasheen James* contains eleven stories about the redoubtable character, based pretty closely on the real life Tom O'Gorman who did from time to time take up residence in the shed at the bottom of Walsh's garden. Once created, of course, the fictional character and the real soon diverged. But Thomasheen James was hugely popular at the time, particularly in America. The stories are light, amusing pieces but little more.

Son of a Tinker contains the story of that name and eight others of which the best is certainly *The Bonesetter*, set in Ireland in the days of George III and about a man with a gift for healing and a deadly sword. Another fine story in this collection is *My Fey Lady* which tells of a three hundred year old wrong put right at last by the faith of a woman sib to the plea from her foremother of old time. The collection as a whole is mixed but there are certainly some excellent examples of the storyteller at his best.

The Honest Fisherman has six stories, two of them about Thomasheen James. The two most effective tales are *The Sword of Yung-lo* which is a variant of the worm turning theme, with a tinge of magic about the sword itself, and *Take Your Choice* which presents an interesting twist to the fairy godmother theme.

The Smart Fellow was the collection on which Walsh was working when he died. There are seven finished stories, three about Thomasheen James and of the rest the best is *The Missing Meerschaum*, a quite hilarious tale of heaven and hell and the keepers of the many different gates of Heaven.

The final group contains the two detective stories Walsh wrote:

| *The Man in Brown* | (1945) |
| *Danger under the Moon* | (1956). |

Walsh himself enjoyed detective stories, like his father before him, and it was not surprising that he should try his hand at the form. The two books are well enough constructed but it was not his metier and he himself was not pleased with them.

Conclusion

First and last Walsh was a storyteller in a vivid mould. His gift – and it was considerable – was to make vision and reality coalesce in the mind of his reader, to make the hills and glens, rivers and lochs, breathe and live and to people them with strong, engaging, quirky, lovable, laughable, fearsome, convincing, interesting characters. His ear was acute for the niceties of speech and his dialogues and conversations ring true, from the tinker to the earl.

But precise and careful though he was about the details of speech, it is his prose which reveals how naturally storytelling came to him. He himself said of writing:

"It takes a little practise but not much. The secret is proper visualization – a good sense of sound and colour."[1]

A typically modest statement. But it is clear that as his skill with word pictures sharpened and was steadily refined, Walsh evolved a simple, direct style which was immediately appealing. He was able to ramble and seemingly digress but in the manner of the accomplished speaker who departs from his main theme but never loses sight of it. The approach was very effective.

The content of his books was essentially wholesome and he would have been delighted to have them described as "entertainments" though some went far beyond that. His themes were romantic in a visionary and wholly honourable

---

[1] Letter to his niece, 7.10.41.

sense, adventurous in a vivid, exciting, forthright way. He made particularly telling use of the return of the native or the arrival of the stranger to precipitate action but the action thus set in train would be honourable in intention and execution.

Bryan MacMahon made the telling point, as usual, when he told me that for him the image he got from the books was essentially that of the man himself. I understood at once. There was about the man and his works a sense of wholeness, excitement and tolerance which accounts for the wide appeal of his stories. The man himself was quite exceptionally engaging and the force of his own personality shines through many of his characters.

The books vary considerably in quality. Some are indeed no more than amusing entertainments. Others stand with the best there is. But all in varying degrees have delicacy and understanding, compassion and strength, colour and motion, salt and humour, action and emotion. The characters who populate the books are varied and vivid but it was undoubtedly in the painting of scenes and the building of atmosphere that Walsh's brightest and strongest talents showed themselves. His books breathe the open air, the clean, shrivening, soul clearing, mind and spirit lifting air of the Highlands of Scotland and the west of Ireland. His stage was mountain and stream, hill and glen in Moray and in Kerry. The pages of his books take their strength from the wide outdoors and the high ideals of the people he found there. Strong, fine, open places with high hills, soaring vistas and wide horizons often do produce people of rare quality. Maurice Walsh was one of them.

THOMAS MACGREEVY: THE MAN AND HIS WORK
BY JOHN COOLAHAN

Introduction

It is very appropriate that Listowel Writers' Week should commemorate the life and work of this remarkable North Kerryman. This is because of the many significant contributions MacGreevy has made to the arts, through his poetry, his literary and artistic criticism, through his friendship and help to some of the greatest artists of this century and through his promotion of the arts in Ireland. MacGreevy was the respected friend and confidant of some of the great international artists of the century and was at home in many of the great art centres of Europe. But he combined this with a rootedness in Ireland and, in particular, in North Kerry. In the opening pages of his memoirs, written during his last years, he wrote, ". . . the reality of North Kerry has been in the background at all times since I first left it."[1]

The literary link with the area and with Listowel remained imprinted in his memory. His description of his first visit as a boy to the delights of Flavin's bookshop in Listowel is so graphic that it is worth quoting at some length:

On the day of my first visit to Listowel (for music lessons) I made a life-long friend, a man who deserves to be remembered as one of the greatest booksellers that Ireland has ever known . . . Having entered the shop suddenly Mr. Flavin the bookseller himself was at my side, reddish haired, strong jawed, smiling down at me with the dancing eyes of a John Fitzgerald, and asking questions. After a few moments he said "Come and I'll show you books, son," and taking my hand he led me upstairs . . . "Choose what books you want in there, you know the way down," and still smiling, he left me.

---

[1] Thomas MacGreevy, *Memoirs* (unpublished), p. 3.

I chose only such books as I could afford to pay for and I was soon down in the shop again. "Is that all you took?" the smiling man exclaimed. Holding out my hand with the shilling, which was all the money I had, I tried to explain. But he closed my hand over the money and said, "the books are yours, son". From that day on, over the forty years or more that he lived, I seldom or never passed through Listowel without calling to see Mr. Flavin.[1]

This is a lovely tribute to Mr. Flavin and his Listowel bookshop and also a reminder of the quiet way in which talents may be fostered by good bookshops and good booksellers in many small towns. It was Dan Flavin who drew the attention of Bryan MacMahon to MacGreevy and fostered a deeply held friendship. MacGreevy wrote of the bond between two of them in this way:

> Bryan MacMahon, for all his international fame, remains
> very much a Listowel man and his goodness and
> generous friendship make me feel that the literary links
> with Listowel and the world of my youth remain
> unbroken.[2]

I think Tom MacGreevy would be deeply pleased at our presence here, as part of Listowel Writers' Week, to endorse the enduring character of those links and to show that his work has not been forgotten by his own people.

There is yet a further aspect of the appropriateness of our commemoration in that the lecture is being held under the aegis of the Seamus Wilmot memorial lecture sequence. Again, according to MacGreevy, it was Dan Flavin who first drew the attention of Seamus Wilmot to an article of MacGreevy's in the early 1920's and, again, links were established between these local writers. For many years they did not have far to go to have a chat when MacGreevy

---

[1] Memoirs., pp. 70, 71.

[2] Ibid., pp. 75.

presided as Director of the National Gallery in Merrion Square while, across the square, his fellow North Kerryman, Dr. Seamus Wilmot, guided the affairs of the National University of Ireland, as Registrar. Even so, Tom MacGreevy and Seamus Wilmot set time apart for more extended discussion and they met regularly on Sunday mornings in the Gresham Hotel, sometimes joined by interested friends.

Thus, for many reasons I esteem it a privilege to be asked to speak on Thomas MacGreevy in Listowel, at Writers' Week, on the occasion of the Seamus Wilmot Memorial Lecture.

MacGreevy's Career and Life's Work

Thomas MacGreevy was born in Tarbert in 1893, the seventh child of a local national school teacher and a retired R.I.C. policeman. In his memoirs he evokes with astonishing detail his happy childhood in Tarbert. Like his great friends of later life W.B. Yeats, Joyce and Beckett, a sense of place, imbibed during the impressionable years of childhood and youth, was of great significance for MacGreevy's consciousness. He bore fond remembrances of Tarbert:

> It is not only the wooded hills rising from
> the estuary of the Shannon shores towards
> distant mountains that help to make it beautiful.
> The villa-like residences and even the farmhouses
> are in architectural harmony with the natural
> scene.[1]

He loved the house where he grew up on the Glin Road, with its books, its music, and its spacious rear garden, verging down to the bay. He was very open to the beauty of the varied local landscape. He wrote of the boglands of Dooncaha,

---

[1] Memoir p. 10.

The colour of the sunlit bogland stretching
westwards to Knockanore Hill, twelve miles away,
was beautiful even to the eyes of a small boy,
and that small boy could appreciate, as the
aging man still does, the keen freshness of the air
blowing in from the Atlantic and Knockanore.[1]

However, he rightly concluded that while he loved the beauty of the natural bogland, footing turf was not to be his forte!

He wrote movingly, and in detail, of his activity as an altar boy, visits to the outlying houses for the "stations', with the dignified parish priest, Fr. Foley. MacGreevy recalls the internal features and beauty of the old Tarbert church, its statues, sanctuary, memorial tablets, etc. in stunning detail and is surely correct in his conclusion that they helped "the developing visual sense of at least one small boy."[2]

The Old Franciscan Abbey at Lislaughlin he admired for its architecture; it was long to haunt his work for its symbolic import. Open to colour, sounds, illustrations and various manifestations of beauty around him, the young MacGreevy was storing up an artistic sensibility which was later to blossom into a recognised connoisseurship over a range of arts. In his memoirs he posed and answered a question on this theme:

It might well be asked whether, in the matter of the fine arts, the circumstances of my childhood in a remote Irish village contributed towards the more or less amateur humanism, to which in my old age, I may perhaps claim to have attained. Well believe it or not, they did.[3]

Having completed the full progamme of national school, the young MacGreevy studied in Tarbert privately and sat

---

[1] Memoirs p. 13.
[1] Ibid., p. 82.
[3] Ibid., p. 77.

for, and was successful in the civil service examinations. This involved a shift to Dublin, where, largely prompted by his own interests, he began a lifelong association with the insides of art galleries, attended plays, concerts and opera in the capital city. The foundations were being secured for his very wide-ranging interest in the arts. His transfer to London to work in the war-time admirality section of the civil service allowed him even greater opportunity to extend his experience and deepen his appreciation of the arts in one of the greatest art centres of the world. This was an opportunity he explored to the full. One of the most illuminating of these experiences was his encounter with a Giorgione painting "Shepherd with a pipe" in Hampton Court Palace. Giorgione was to be one of the great influences on his artistic consciousness throughout life – "It was never to lose its hold on me." He called it "a day of days" in which he had found

> a spirit, a temper, a human approach in
> which dream and reality, imagination and
> intellect, the transcendent and the
> immanent seemed in perfect felicity, ideally,
> divinely as it might be, to blend.[1]

Meanwhile, on the fields of Flanders and the trenches of the Somme, a very different scene was being acted out, as the Great War dragged on and much of a generation was lost in the mire of the western front. MacGreevy volunteered for the war effort about January 1917 and took on the rather unlikely role of gunner in an artillery regiment. His memoirs reflect a remarkable degree of detail in his recollections of life among the troops in war-time France. One striking incident he recalls from the Salient of Ypres was the shooting down of an English plane "and its descent in flames inside the German lines on a morning of brilliant sunshine which I recalled in my poem *De Civitate Hominum*",[2] a

---

[1] *Memoirs*, p. 253.
[1] Ibid., p. 345.

poem characterised by Anthony Cronin as "one of the finest and least known poetic products of the holocaust".[1] MacGreevy was wounded twice, the second occasion requiring his transfer back to England for medical treatment. Eventually, the war ended and MacGreevy left the army.

Because of his active involvement in the war MacGreevy became eligible for a scholarship which he took up as a mature student of twenty-five at Trinity College Dublin. He took his B.A. in history and politics. While away, he had been relatively unaware of the significance of the 1916 Rising and the stirrings towards a war of independence. However, when he became more informed about the militant nationalist movement his allegiance swung behind it. He took no military role but his sympathies became strongly nationalist and remained so throughout his lifetime, sprinkled with elements of Anglophobia.

He renewed his acquaintance with the artistic and cultural life of Dublin. He involved himself in the Dublin Drama League and the Dublin Arts Club. He wrote for various publications particularly the *Irish Statesman*, and *The Leader* and *New Ireland*. He made the acquaintance and gave support to artists such as Evie Hone, Harry Clarke, Sarah Pursur and Mainie Jellet. He supported the Irish stained glass movement of the period and retained his enthusiasm for it throughout his life. He became close friends with W.B. Yeats and his wife George. He was also friends with Lennox Robinson and resigned his job as a librarian with the Carnegie Foundation in principled support of Robinson, following the latter's dismissal from the library service. He was co-founder, with Robinson and Christina Keogh, of the Irish Central Library for Students.

In May 1924 he made his first visit to Spain and, in 1925, one to Switzerland. His visit to Spain inspired three of his greatest poems, *Aodh Rua O Domhnaill*, *Homage to Hieronymous Bosch* and *Gloria de Carlos V*, while his visit to Switzerland prompted the beautiful, evocative poem *Recessional* which made such an impact later on the

---

[1] Anthony Cronin, *Heritage Now* (Brandon, 1982 p. 56)

American poet, Wallace Stevens. In 1925 he moved to London. With a warm introduction from W.B. Yeats he called on T.S. Eliot and the rather aloof Eliot became friends with MacGreevy. He became a critic for Eliot's journal *The Criterion* and he also wrote on books, art and ballet for the *Times Literary Supplement* and *Athenaeum*. He wrote and got poems published periodically. He also gave lectures at the National Gallery of London. He was appointed assistant editor of the arts journal, *The Connoisseur*.

He seemed, then, well set up in the London arts and journalistic world but he hankered after Paris. Due to his contacts with Trinity College, he was offered the post of English lecturer in the prestigious École Normale Superieure of Paris University and he eagerly accepted this post in 1927, and retained it for four years. Tom loved Paris and came to have a great affinity with the French language and culture which remained with him until his death. Paris was a writer's and artist's paradise in those years. MacGreevy wrote of this period – "My years at the École Normale count among the happiest of my whole life".[1]

He became a close friend of James Joyce, then a presiding giant in Paris literary circles. MacGreevy with a talent for recognising genius, greatly admired Joyce's work, was a regular visitor to the Joyces and was a great favourite with Nora Barnacle. He helped Joyce with proof-reading and aspects of *Finnegans Wake*. The bond between the two men was close and MacGreevy was chosen by Joyce to be his literary executor. In 1928 a rather introverted ex-Trinity man arrived as a lecturer at the École Normale, Samuel Beckett. MacGreevy befriended him and an extraordinary close relationship developed between the two, which lasted until MacGreevy's death, almost forty years later. Beckett's biographer declared that "MacGreevy became Beckett's closest friend and for the rest of his life, Beckett's only confidant."[2] Over 300 letters between Beckett to MacGreevy

---

[1] *Memoirs*, Vol. II, p. 4.
[2] Deirdre Bair, *Samuel Beckett* (Jonathan Cape, 1978), p. 63.

are extent and indicate how fully and deeply Beckett confided in MacGreevy.

MacGreevy was glad to introduce Beckett to Joyce from which a very interesting artistic relationship developed. Both Beckett and MacGreevy were contributors to *Our Exagmination Round his Factification for Incamination of Work in Progress*, a series of essays on the evolving *Finnegans Wake*, published in 1929. Both of them were also guests at the famous Ulysses lunch in June 1929, to celebrate both the French translation of Ulysses and the twenty-fifth anniversary of Bloomsday in June 1904. There, too, was the French poet Paul Valery whose work *Introduction to the Method of Leonardo de Vinci* was translated by MacGreevy into English, in that same year, 1929, which greatly pleased Valery.

MacGreevy also introduced Beckett to T.S. Eliot, who continued to like MacGreevy's company and criticism in the early thirties. However, no friendship blossomed between Eliot and Beckett. A more important introduction by MacGreevy was his arranging for Beckett to meet Jack B. Yeats. All through the years Jack B. remained a very close friend of MacGreevy's, who championed his work in the European arena. This sense of trust was again exemplified by the fact that Jack B. also appointed MacGreevy to be his executor (Yeats died in 1957). Beckett immediately formed a great regard for Yeats who became a most influential model of artistic integrity for Beckett.[1]

In 1930 MacGreevy resigned from École Normale and became assistant editor of *Formes*, an influential journal of fine arts. He wrote articles and poems for many journals. In the spring of 1931 Chatto and Windus published MacGreevy's *T.S. Eliot: A Study*. In this early study of Eliot, MacGreevy had many interesting comments to make and the influence of Eliot on his own work was also to be important. Yeats wrote to Tom in March 1931 expressing his pleasure in the book:

---

[1] Eoin O'Brien, *The Beckett Country* (The Black Cat Press and Faber and Faber,1986), pp. 281-285

My dear MacGreevy – I am entirely delighted with your essay on Eliot – it is rambling, passionate, crabbed and lucid, and what could a man ask for more? You have said things about passage after passage that I felt when I first read the poems without discovering fitting words. Your prose has a quality of momentum which has for some time been fading out of prose and verse alike . . .[1]

Eliot must have liked the work also, despite its criticism of "Ash Wednesday", because shortly after the book was published he wrote to MacGreevy inviting him to visit him in London and signing the letter "your obliged obedient servant T.S. Eliot".[2] In September 1931 another study by MacGreevy in the same Dolphin series appeared – *Richard Aldington: An Englishman*. This was a favourable appreciation of the poet and novelist. MacGreevy and Aldington became friends, with MacGreevy accompanying Aldington on trips to Italy and its art galleries. In his autobiography Aldington recalled ". . . there never was a more good-humoured fellow-traveller or one who gave more by communicating a fine appreciation".[3] (Deirdre Bair reported that several decades later, about 1960, when MacGreevy met Aldington in Southern Europe, the latter was in spare circumstances, he communicated this to Beckett who sent financial assistance, in remembrance of early help by Aldington to him.)[4]

Throughout the thirties MacGreevy made many trips to European art centres, although he was not well off. These were years when he expanded on his first-hand knowledge

---

[1] Letter from W.B. Yeats to MacGreevy, 10 Mar. 1931 quoted in Schreibman, P. XIX.

[2] Quoted in Susan Schreibman "Weeping over a lost Poetry": an Annotated Edition of Collected Poems of Thomas MacGreevy (unpublished M.A. Thesis, U.C.D. 1985, p. XIX).

[3] Quoted by Schreibhman, op. cit. p. XXI

[4] Bair, *Samuel Beckett*, p. 511

of many of the great paintings in European galleries. At this period he fitted the part in which he characterises himself in his late book on Poussin when he stated, "I was the modern equivalent of the roving poor scholar of Irish tradition".[1] There were other roving Irish scholars who gravitated to Paris in the thirties. Among the many, befriended and assisted by MacGreevy, were the two young Irish poets Denis Devlin and Brian Coffey, who retained warm regard for him.

Tom MacGreevy moved back to London in 1933, where in 1934, his volume of *Poems* was published by Heinemann. Some of the poems had already appeared in *The Irish Statesman* (Dublin) *Transition* and *The New Review* (Paris); *The Criterion* and *The Dublin Review* (London); and *The Dial* (New York). The dust jacket to this collection of thirty-one poems, in my view, felicitously catches their character:

> Here is an Irish poet whose work is never provincial, but always in close touch with the European Catholic tradition. These poems are sensitive, subtle and allusive; new word patterns, some of which are direct, while the thought and meaning of others are gradually revealed as one broods over their complicated musical structure. They are the work of a poet whose intellectual delicacy often implies far more than it states . . .[2]

Regrettably, this was to be the last volume of poetry published by him and when his *Collected Poems* were published by New Writers' Press in 1971 they contained only five extra poems.

MacGreevy resumed his lecturing at the National Gallery in London and translated works of Henri de Montherlant, Ella Maillary and Marthe Bibesco. During these years he also wrote a large part of his study of the painting of Jack B. Yeats, but failed to get an English publisher, which may

---

[1] Thomas MacGreevy, *Nicholas Poussin*, *Dolmen Press*, 1960, p. iv.

[2] Thomas MacGreevy, *Poems*, Heinemann, 1934.

have been partly due to some anti-English sentiments it contained but, perhaps, also a reluctance to acknowledge the genius of Jack Yeats' work.

In 1939, just 21 years after "the war to end all wars," the hounds of war were again unleashed, in a conflict that waged far and wide for six years and bought great disillusionment to those who cherished the values of European civilization. In 1941 MacGreevy returned to Dublin. Dublin was to remain his base until his death in 1967, with periodical forays to Paris, to foreign art exhibitions, and meetings of international art critics.

It is not at all clear that the rather introverted Dublin of the 1940's was a suitable milieu for a talent such as MacGreevy's. In any case, the somewhat bohemian character of his early life was abandoned as he settled in Dublin. It should be remembered that, unlike Joyce and Beckett who distanced themselves from Catholicism and Irish nationalism, MacGreevy embraced both enthusiastically, which made living in Dublin more congenial to him. He began writing many articles on the arts and artists for journals such as *The Capuchin Annual* and *The Father Matthew Record*. Between 1942 and 1965 he wrote twenty four pieces for *The Capuchin Annual*, and fifty for *The Record*, between 1941 and 1953. While interesting and informative to Irish readers the quality of these articles was uneven. He tried to open Irish eyes to the work of Irish and European artists, but he lacked an international audience, both in terms of receptivity and of critical standards.

A work of more enduring significance was his completed study *Jack B. Yeats: An Appreciation and an Interpretation,* published in Dublin in 1945. The same year saw his publication, *The Pictures in the National Gallery* by Batsford in London.

The Second World War ended in 1945 and Europe, in the wake of the defeat of fascism, began its economic and cultural re-construction. In this renewal of European cultural life MacGreevy was gratified, in 1948, when the French Government honoured him by making him a Chevalier of the Legion of Honour, for his services to the arts. National recognition followed shortly afterwards when, in 1950, he was appointed Director of the National Art Gallery. No other position could have pleased him more. He was also appointed to the Arts Council on its foundation in 1951. This heralded a decade which gave him much pleasure in his work and many public honours.

In 1954 he made his only visit to America, as a guest at the Metropolitan Art Gallery in New York. He had a memorable four hour meeting there with the poet Wallace Stevens, with whom he had established a remarkable correspondence relationship since 1948. Stephens wrote "I love to have his friendship and goodwill".[1] MacGreevy influenced Stephens in a number of ways and quite directly in three poems and two major essays. In 1948, Stevens wrote the poem, "Tom MacGreevy in America, thinks of himself as a boy". In the course of this poem Stevens, while influenced by MacGreevy's, *Recessional*, adapts lines from his Bosch poem so that Stevens asserts that it is the poetry of home, the sound of Tarbert, that MacGreevy hears in the Dublin wind. Stevens's stanza read:

> Over the top of the Bank of Ireland,
> The wind blows quaintly
> Its thin stringed music
> As he heard it in Tarbert.[2]

In 1956 MacGreevy published his *Catalogue of the Italian Paintings* and was honoured by the Italian Government with the Cavaliere Ufficiale al Merito. The following year 1957, the Senate of the National University of Ireland, at the instigation of MacGreevy's friend, the fine scholar and gentleman, Monsignor Pádraig de Brún, conferred Thomas MacGreevy with its honorary Doctorate of Letters. His health was disimproving in these years and it was while recuperating from a heart attack in 1958, that he

---

[1] Quoted in Schreibman, op. cit., p. xxii.
[2] Peter Brazeau, "The Irish Connection: Wallace Stevens and Thomas MacGreevy", *The Southern Review* XVII (Summer, 1981), pp. 533 - 41

wrote his study of the seventeenth century French artist, Nicolas Poussin, one of the few studies of a major European artist published in Dublin.

It gave him great pleasure in 1962 to organise the Jack B. Yeats exhibition for the great international exhibition at the Venice Biennale. This great Yeats exhibition was mounted in Dublin in November 1962. Also in 1962 the French Government again honoured Tom by raising him to the status of Officer of the Legion of Honour. In 1963 he published *Some Italian Pictures in the National Gallery* and the Italian Government was pleased to award him its silver cultural medal in recognition of his services to Italian art. Also, in 1963, he published his important *Concise Catalogue of the Oil Paintings in the National Gallery*. He was now battling with ill health and he retired from the Gallery in 1963. During his last years he worked on his memoirs which he showed to Samuel Beckett on the latter's last visit to him in Dublin in 1966. Thomas MacGreevy died peacefully while reading a book on the eve of St. Patrick's Day 1967, following a life of rich and varied experience, stretching from his childhood in Tarbert in the last years of the old century, through the more turbulent, but artistically exciting two thirds of the twentieth century.

MacGreevy's Literary Work

MacGreevy's literary work was of varied character. Some consisted of a variety of articles on writers, artists and current affairs in a wide range of Irish and foreign journals such as *The Irish Statesman, The Criterion, The Times Literary Supplement, The Connoisseur, Forbes, Transition, The Capuchin Annual, Fr. Matthew Record* and so on. He also wrote a perceptive study of George Moore in *Scrutinies.*

His translation of Valery was important but his other translations were of a routine character. His literary studies of T.S. Eliot and Aldington were significant appreciations of these key writers at the time they were published, in 1931. They are still worth reading and they reflect a discriminating taste in MacGreevy coupled with his skill in identifying writers of significance and his support of the avant-garde in literature, as well as painting, music and ballet. He assisted

Joyce in a number of ways and contributed an essay *The Catholic Element in Work in Progress* to the compilation on that work in 1929. MacGreevy was of crucial importance to Beckett and acted as reader for Beckett's works, giving particular encouragement to the novel *Murphy*, at a time when this was important to the writer.

However, MacGreevy's real literary importance is based on his poems, the first Irish poet in the modern idiom *à la* Eliot and Pound rather than Yeats. It is his poetry that is of particular importance for Writer's Week and one would suggest that a session in a future Writers' Week programme might be devoted to a specialist study of his poetry. What MacGreevy represents in the development of Irish poetry is of real and lasting significance. He is a vital link in the shift from the Yeatsian mode to the modern mode of the poets of the thirties. But, more importantly, his poems are of enduring worth and beauty in themselves.

On this occasion I will just draw attention to the regard in which some other Irish writers hold MacGreevy's poetry. In his incisive review of *Poems* in 1934, entitled "Humanistic Quietism", Beckett detected key characteristics of the poems:

It is from this nucleus of endopsychic clarity, uttering itself in the prayer that is a spasm of awareness, and from no more casual source, that Mr. MacGreevy evolves his poems. This is the energy and integrity of Giorgionismo, self-absorption into light.[1]

That he valued the poems highly is clear when Beckett remarked of them:

This is the adult mode of prayer syntonic to Mr. MacGreevy, the unfailing salute to his significant from which the fire is struck and the poem kindled, and

---

[1] S. Beckett, "Humanistic Quietism" in *Disjecta*, Calder, 1983, p. 69.

kindled to a radiance without counterpart in the work of contemporary poets writing in English.[1]

It is noteworthy that this aspect of radiance was the element which struck the Irish composer, Professor Seoirse Bodley when he came across the poems in the 1970s and arranged them as a choral work entitled *The Radiant Moment.*

A fellow poet of the thirties, Brian Coffey, remarks that in *Poems* MacGreevy:

aimed at concision, the words few, the themes selected, historical awareness strengthening the lyrical or satirical movement of the separate poems: all proceeding from a central gentleness, a basic tenderness respectful of the diversity in things, and ready in loving assent to life and death.

He goes on to indicate the qualities MacGreevy brought to bear in his verse:

Musical culture, historical insight and a profound understanding of painting which an exceptional memory for colours underpinned as much as did a vast capacity for facts, added surface and rhythmical variety to MacGreevy's natural disposition for poetry.

He concludes that MacGreevy "was a singularly perfect poet" whose work "is a rare part of our natural literary heritage".[2] A younger poet Basil Payne found the poetry "striking" and held that "Its predominant merits are originality, directness, and more importantly, a genuine responsiveness to rhythm".[3] Anthony Cronin formed a very

---

[1] Ibid., p. 70.

[2] Brian Coffey, "In Tribute to Thomas MacGreevy", *Capuchin Annual* 1968, pp. 278 – 282

[3] Basil Payne, "In Tribute to Thomas MacGreevy", *Capuchin Annual* 1968, pp. 287 - 291.

high opinion of MacGreevy's poetry placing it in the modern tradition:

> To make the claim for MacGreevy that he was one of the very few who were able to write free verse deriving from, but not necessarily imitative of, Eliot is therefore to award an Irish poet of the era a not inconsiderable place in the international scheme of things. But I go, further: MacGreevy wrote, after Eliot himself, the most perfectly modulated free verse written in the period in England, Ireland, or America.

As far as Cronin is concerned,

> Thomas MacGreevy occupies a place of peculiar importance in the history of Irish letters in that he was the first specifically and consciously modern Irish poet.

and he regards some of MacGreevy's poems as "among the best written anywhere in English in this century".[1] Quite clearly, even though MacGreevy's poetry did not enjoy popular acclaim, he holds a high place in the regard of his discriminating peers.

MacGreevy's Art Criticism

Thomas MacGreevy's main works of art criticism are his study of Jack B. Yeats (1945) and of Nicolas Poussin (1960). There are many other essays, the ones on neglected Irish artists – Michael Healy, John Hogan and Patrick Touhy – being particularly interesting. His work on Jack B. Yeats aimed to set Yeats within a context of the great artists of the western tradition. He laid great stress on Yeats as the national painter par excellence,

---

[1] Anthony Cronin, "Thomas MacGreevy, Modernism not Triumphant" in *Heritage Now* (Brandon, 1984), pp. 155 – 160.

who in his work was the consummate
expression of the spirit of his own
nation at one of the supreme points in
its evolution.[1]

He considered that it was through Yeats that after centuries
of repression had brought them down to zero in all the arts,
the underdog, conquered people of Ireland came for the first
time to a measure of self expression in the modern art of
painting.[2] MacGreevy rejoiced in the early works of Yeats
wherein were captured

> the people of Ireland, men, women and children,
> at work and play, farmers, labourers, car-drivers,
> jockeys, ballad-singers, tramps, women old and
> young, barefooted, boys in rakish looking caps.[3]

He loved "the unearthly light and unearthly colours" in
Yeats, and Yeat's horses "of which there were no lovelier in
all painting". MacGreevy also appreciated the changes in
Yeats's style whereby "the knife was frequently substituted
for the brush", and "form is suggested rather than realised,
and colour and movement predominate".[4]

MacGreevy's study of Poussin was also a labour of
love. In the introduction he tells us

> If I had been caught by Giorgione before
> the First World War, the great Nicolas
> had cast his spell on me shortly after it,
> perhaps because of it.[5]

He wrote insightfully on several of Poussin's
masterpieces, including *The Holy Family* and *The*

---

[1] Thomas MacGreevy, *Jack B. Yeats: An Appreciation and an Interpertation* (Waddington, 1945), p. 9.
[2] Ibid., p. 8.
[3] Ibid., p. 22.
[4] Ibid., p. 24 and p. 36.
[5] Thomas MacGreevy, *Nicolas Poussin* (Dolmen Press, 1960), p. vi.

Entombment contained in his own beloved National Gallery. MacGreevy's style of art criticism was personal and subjective and anecdotal. His work is much more in the form of appreciation from a fine poetic sensibility, than that of the academic critic. In Poussin the prose is a very polished, easy-flowing conversational style, which he himself recognised would appeal more to the general reader than to the art historian or man of letters.

MacGreevy as Director of the National Gallery, 1950-1963

His appointment as Director of the National Gallery was the fulfilment of a long-held ambition for MacGreevy, as he noted in his memoirs, "I had loved the place since I first visited it in 1910".[1] He had applied for the job in 1927 and was second to his friend Thomas Bodkin, out of seventeen applicants.[2] He was also unsuccessful when Furlong was appointed in 1935. When MacGreevy was appointed in June 1950, his appointment coincided with some happy auguries for the future of the Gallery. One was the arrival of Sir Chester Beatty the great art collector, to settle in Dublin in June 1950. As might be expected, with MacGreevy's background and quite extraordinary flair for conversation and friendship both men became close friends, which was no hindrance to the many bequests which Chester Beatty made to the Gallery. Both men were also appointed to the newly established Arts Council in 1951, which probably was a factor in that body's emphasis on the fine arts in its early history. Another happy augury for the Gallery was the announcement by Bernard Shaw, in April 1950, that the National Gallery was being designated as a beneficiary in his will.

MacGreevy was concerned to extend the Gallery, brighten its facilities and make it a more attractive venue for the general public. He was considerably successful in this

---

[1] *Memoirs*, Vol. II, p. 1.
[2] Letter from W.B. Yeats to MacGreevy, 1927.

and the image changed from being a quiet retreat for art lovers and refined and genteel Dubliners to being a more active, open institution, a foundation which was splendidly built on by James White, MacGreevy's successor. MacGreevy submitted his request for an extension of the Gallery to the Board in 1951, but the 1950s were not a propitious period for public expenditure in the arts. Nevertheless, MacGreevy had the satisfaction in 1962, before his retirement, to have his extension plans accepted and his advice on the new extension helped to make it the impressive success that it is.

When he assumed office in 1950 the post of Director was a part-time one, but he got this changed to a full-time position, with secretarial assistance in 1956, and he also got an assistant director appointed. As part of his concern to open up the gallery, he established a panel of paid lecturers to deliver free public lectures on the treasures of the collections. He introduced the first of a large series of coloured postcards of the paintings for sale to the general public and, before his retirement in 1963, he commissioned a series of coloured slides. In 1963, he also published his *Some Italian Pictures* in the National Gallery and *The Concise Catalogue of the Oil Painting*. He initiated moves for the establishment of a Restoration Department in the Gallery, which has since become a great success.

Most importantly, MacGreevy made some valuable purchases for the Gallery's collections, often at very low prices. He had his disappointments, and he regretted the Board's refusal to accept his advice to purchase an Ingres painting and a Raphael portrait. However, he also had his successes and among his notable purchases were the great Murillos and the El Mudo, as well as Tintoretto's *Venice Crowing the Adriatic*, which was the first painting bought out of the Shaw Fund, when it had become available in 1958. This fund opened up the way for many important acquistions in subsequent years.

MacGreevy was very keen on keeping Irish eyes opened to the international art arena. He was the key originator of the Irish Association of Art Critics and sought to promote art criticism generally in the society. As chairman, and with

James White as secretary, he succeeded in getting the International Congress of Art Critics held in Dublin in 1953. These international links were important on a range of fronts. It must have given Tom rare pleasure, in 1962, to bring the work of his friend Jack B. Yeats, whom he regarded as an artist of international significance, to the City of Venice whose galleries of old masters had so enthralled him as a young man. He also supported the living art movement in Ireland. Failing health led MacGreevy to retire from the National Gallery in 1963, by which time he was seventy years of age. His withdrawal from the Gallery was greatly regretted by the staff, to whom his kindness was legendary.

MacGreevy: The Man

When one comes to sum up the kind of man Tom MacGreevy was, this theme of kindness is very relevant. He was a very generous and even unworldly figure for whom money meant little, and there were periods of his life indeed, when he had little. He loved giving and helping and one wonders in this regard if he was influenced by the values of his beloved St. Francis. My first personal recollections of him were when I was a child meeting this dignified figure with the, to me, unusal "dicky-bow", on his walks to the Back of the Hill and Tarbert Island. He gave me the feeling of gentleness then, and later when I got to know him better in the early sixties in Dublin this feeling was confirmed. I ran a poetic theatre group in Dublin – The Seagull Poetic Theatre – with an interest in the poetic drama of Yeats, Clarke, Maeterlink, Lorca, Sophocles, and Tom MacGreevy was most interested and supportive, perhaps recollecting his own enthusiasms and involvements in the early twenties. He secured us guarantees against loss from the Arts Council, made contributions from his own pocket and attended regularly at productions, even though his health was failing. He wrote long interesting letters on how to present the Greek choruses and so on. We never did accede to his request to put on Jack Yeats' *La La Noo* or *In Sand*.

MacGreevy's manners and manner were of an older, more dignified and gracious world than the casual and more brash behaviour of more recent decades. He dressed formally and was exceedingly courteous and refined in his mode of address. Dr. MacGreevy was a man of sensitive temperament which would, one suspects, be vulnerable to conscious or unconscious slights inflicted by others. He was most at home in the company of artists, writers and aesthetes. From a wide range of sources one gathers that he was a brilliant conversationalist who loved to draw on a wide range of ancedotes, references, events and places from his well-stored memory. He had this gift of sparkling conversation from his early years and extant letters testify how much his company was sought by the Yeatses, A.E., Eliot, Aldington, Joyce, and so on. In later years, in Dublin, he was a welcome guest at many tables where, in intimate gatherings of like-minded people, he entertained his audience with his conversational gifts.

Linked to this, was MacGreevy's gift of reaching out to people and forming loyal and lasting friendships. The fact that he was confided in and trusted by artists as individual and, in ways, as self-centred as Joyce, Beckett and Jack Yeats is eloquent witness to his quality as a friend. MacGreevy exhibited another striking trait, again reflective of older social conventions and that is his quite extraordinary skill as correspondent or letter writer. The volume of his letters was prodigious. One of the more remarkable literary correspondences of the century was his correspondence with Wallace Stevens. His correspondence to a range of other artists is of considerable interest to students of twentieth century arts and literature.

One of the most disturbing unanswered questions about MacGreevy is why, having written some excellent poetry by 1934, he largely ceased to do so subsequently. A number of reasons may be put forward. The lack of popular success and recognition must have been a great disappointment to him in the thirties. There is a poignancy in his early poem *Nocturne* when borne in mind about his poetry:

> I labour in a barren place
> Alone, self-conscious, frightened, blundering;
> Far away, stars wheeling in space,
> About my feet, earth voices whispering.

Dublin in the 1940s was not a congenial or supportive environment for poetry of MacGreevys idiom.

However, MacGreevy may also have lacked the sustained discipline and staying power for the difficult process of creative writing. He, himself, hints at this in his *Memoirs* when he reflects:

> There was a time when I dreamed of being a writer. As the things worked out I never became more than a part-time writer. That could be due to economic circumstance. It could be due as well to my psychological make-up. I think I may say that I have always been as much interested in living as in writing about living.

He went on to contrast Sam Beckett's approach to his own in Paris, in the early years:

> When, for a time at the Èlcole Normale and later, for a short period at a hotel in the Quarter, Samuel Beckett and I had adjoining rooms and breakfasted together, Sam could go straight from his morning tea or coffee to his typewriter or his books . . . I, on the contrary, had to go out and make sure that the world was where I had left it the evening before. What is more, it was only a possibility that I would go back and work for myself during the day. I wrote best in the stillness of the night when there was no outside work to be done and nobody left to talk to.[1]

Tom was a compulsive talker and of a very gregarious disposition. He may have given in to the temptation of avoiding the loneliness and pain of the serious creative writer's desk.

Aldington in his autobiography seems to make a perceptive comment when he remarks:

---

[1] *Memoirs*, pp. 1, 2.

Tom MacGreevy had all the gifts of a writer, except the urge to write . . . His creative impulse was satisfied by the undoubted influence his talk had on a sympathetic audience, and that is the danger of having the gift of conversation. Moreover, Tom is the kind of man whose brains are picked by other people.[1]

Indeed, it is true to say that MacGreevy was a great facilitator and promoter of other peoples' talents. As early as 1930, Aldington warned MacGreevy of his tendency not to get down to sustained creative work. He wrote "You have about three times as much talent as I have, and you wrap your talent in a napkin. Beware of Judgement Day".[2]

However much we may regret that Tom MacGreevy did not leave us a greater legacy of exquisite poems, I do not think he need have feared the Lord's judgement as to the employment of his talents. He may not have had the single-minded dedication often necessary in an artist, and which his friends Beckett and Jack B, had in abundance. But he did employ his manifold talents in a variety of directions and most unselfishly. Tom MacGreevy was a man of a deeply religious cast of mind. Shortly before his death, in the last completed pages of his memoirs, his mind turned again, as it had in the beginning of the memoirs, to his North Kerry roots: "I think the values of my North Kerry upbringing always retained their validity for me".[3] As we bade farewell to Tom in Mount Jerome Cemetary, on that March day in 1967 a wreath was delivered from his old mate, Sam Beckett, – The Chevalier had left the stage, having bade his last adieu.

---

[1] Quoted Schreibman, op. cit., p. xxi.

[2] Schreibman, op. cit., p. xxii.

[3] *Memoirs*, Vol. II, p. 5.

GEORGE FITZMAURICE (1877-1963)
(From the original portrait by Harry Kernoff. Copied by permission of
Micheál Ó hAodha. (Photo — courtesy of the Irish Times)

MAURICE WALSH (1879-1964)
(Photo - courtesy of Manus Walsh)

THOMAS MacGREEVY (1893-1967)
(Photo — courtesy of the Irish Times)

BRYAN MacMAHON
(Photo: Brendan Landy)

JOHN B. KEANE
(Photo: Brendan Landy)

BRENDAN KENNELLY

GABRIEL FITZMAURICE
(Photo: Stella Downey)

THE FABULOUS REALISM OF BRYAN MACMAHON

BY AUGUSTINE MARTIN

Here's a tale of the Irish roads, of a tinker and his wife.
It's a tale of trouble and wildness and a child that's born
 to life.
There's mating in it, birth and death, and drink to fill a
 dyke;
So here's how they raced the coloured road that led to
 the Honey Spike.

The quintessence of Bryan MacMahon is in these four lines. Energy is at the centre of his creative impulse, order at its perimeters. The young tinker-hero of the *The Honey Spike*, Martin Claffey, has taken his bride to the Giant's Causeway, the "very top of Ireland" to satisfy his sense of wonder and bravado. He must now fight his way back to Kerry to satisfy Breda's mysterious longing to have her child born at the lucky hospital, the "honey spike" in the hills above Kenmare. There is primal mystery in the setting out and the return – mating, birth and death. In between there is the life which the gypsy bride reads on the palm of her hand as they turn their ponycart south: "sky an' sea, starvation and good feeling . . . drink and drought, Christmas an' Easter, love and hate, life an' death." The romance of their northward adventure is ironically mirrored in every step of their desperate journey south through hostile terrain and wintry weather. There is a tragic symmetry in Breda's death at the Honey Spike to the clamour of traditional lamentation:
"Cry her loud an' keen. A woman dead, I tell ye, an' givin' birth to life. So cry her, you gang o' paupers from the pit o' hell."
It is archetypal stuff.
Northrop Frye, scholar of archetypes, divides literary genre into a seasonal pattern. Comedy with its celebration of fertility and young love is the mythos of Spring; romance with its insistence on magic and miracle is the mythos of

Summer; tragedy with its blend of ripeness, decay and death is the mythos of Autumn; satire with its insistence on the dry critical intelligence is the mythos of Winter, and it is least prominent of the four in MacMahon's world. All are encompassed in the tinker ballad, in Breda's prophesy and in the novel's narrative curve. A similar sense of primal energy, cyclical recurrence, the seasonal rhythms of work and play, birth and death enliven MacMahon's exquisite idyll, *Children of the Rainbow*. It is a permanent feature of his short fiction.

Though deeply sophisticated in the technique of the short story, most modern of forms, MacMahon is almost medieval in his sense of natural community, with its trade, tackle and trim, in its endless variety of human types and humours, its drama of transmission by which inherited wisdom passes from one generation to the next, its undefined but implacable sense of order. It was his destiny to have been born in Kerry, a world where that sense of tradition, though especially tenacious, was nevertheless under threat. His short stories enact endless variations on that grand theme. A ground bass of savage nostalgia underlays the social realism with which local character, custom and ritual are reordered and celebrated. However astringent the tone of an individual story one senses the voice of Old Front from *Children of the Rainbow* somewhere in the cellarage:

"Often and often I have told you the kind of place ye were born into. I have striven to raise in ye a pride for the noble people before ye who fell in love with human nature an' through human nature fell in love with God . . . I have striven to convey to you before now that the young life as I lived it was so thronged with small beauties that you wouldn't think it was sons and daughters of the flesh we were but children of the rainbow dwellin' always in the mornin of the world . . . An' if only the all-seein' God had seen fit to send us a man with the gift on ink, then maybe the story of our small wonders would go shoutin' through the borders of the nations." Implicit in Old Font's plea is the fact that only the written, not the spoken word, can avail that culture in its extremity. That is the optimistic, the lyrical side of MacMahon's imagined community. It has darker manifestations which wait for us in ambush at every turn of the fictional road. But there is a real sense in which MacMahon's fiction is an undisguised celebration of Irish pieties in their Listowel colouring. The patriarchal figure of Old Font is ubiquitous in his fictional world, most notably in the figure of Tommy, the Blind Man who supervises the funeral of the story-teller, Peadar Feeney, in *The Good Dead in the Green Hills.*

The *seanchaí* Peadar Feeney, has been entertaining the company at the blind man's house in Friary Lane for decades. The arrival of a radio virtually ends his artistic ministry. The live current of oral tradition is cut off without ceremony or malice, and the old man retreats to his cottage up the street where he lives with his half-witted sister – MacMahon's community contains a medieval, pre-welfare-state variety of human types, the deaf and dumb, the halt, the lame, the mad, the mentally retarded. Years pass, the sister dies unnoticed, the old story-teller falls ill and is taken off to die in the County Home in a town twenty miles distant. When the word comes that Peadar Feeney has died, and that there is no-one to claim his corpse, a tremor of guilt and contrition runs through the company at the blind man's house. The blind man himself rises to the challenge with a kind of prophetic authority that age and traditional knowledge seem to confer in such situations of cultural stress.

The remains are sent for, and arrive by night on a hackney car to his house at Friary Lane. Then the blind man enters upon what turns out to be an extended ceremony of respect and perhaps reparation. He insists that mountings be affixed, at his expense, to the plain coffin. When he discovers that the coffin has not been opened he goes up a note on the scale of his ritual outrage:

" 'Bad messengers! bad messengers! Said the blind man. You should have asked to see his face.'
Jack-the-Turkey was porter-valiant. 'Admittin' that we didn't see him – an' what did that signify?'
Up blazed the ready anger of the blind man. 'What did that signify? In God's name are ye stumps of fools? How do

we know that it isn't an old fisherman from the west ye brought home to us an not our own Peadar Feeney?' "
His anger mounts as his fingers test the cheap shroud in which the corpse is dressed.
" 'No holy picture either,' he said, 'no tassels!' His left hand was on the lining of the coffin . . . 'Ho! Sixpenny cotton and sawdust. God help the poor, the rich can beg!' Then with an intensity as the fingers of the right hand probed deeper into the habit, 'Nothing next the corpse's skin. God again help the poor.' " He sends, at his own expense for a new habit and underclothes, and when the corpse is decently dressed he twines his own rosary beads round the dead man's hands. The story ends with the blind man and the youngster who tells the story leading the funeral: "Behind us I could hear the men changing fours frequently and even jostling subdudely for places under the coffin'. In the last line he records his pride 'that I was the leader of all those beautiful people.'

The story enacts a ritual in which Friary Lane asserts itself as a community, atoning for a wrong against an oral tradition which is splendid but doomed. For an evening a past glory is revived and honoured in the throes of its obsolescence. Though the writer does not formally acknowledge it, a whole folk culture has come to grief by the story's end; the mourners will assemble the following night around their wireless in the blind man's house; soon it will be the television and the video. These and other questions are not allowed to arise. Ireland's legendary habit of honouring the dead while neglecting the living may occur to the reader's mind, but without apparent prompting from the author. The suppressed birth-pangs of modernity beneath the story's narrative ease are not allowed to surface. It is enough for the moment that a man 'with the gift of ink' has tenderly recorded the old world in its final rites of passage.

The dramatising of communal emotion is notably the province of the drama from *Oedipus Rex* through *Murder in the Cathedral* to *The Crucible*. Hugo, Tolstoy, Dickens, Hawthorne, George Moore and Faulkner have managed to accomodate it to the larger perspectives of the historical novel. O'Flaherty achieved it once in *Going into Exile* and

O'Connor in *On the Train,* but these are exceptions in the
short story form. MacMahon, on the other hand, repeatedly
sets himself this almost impossible task. In *The Dancer's
Aunt* the class barriers of an entire town are transcended in
the beauty with which a little girl dances at a parish-hall
concert; in *Island Funeral* the burial of a woman who had
died on the mainland giving birth to her tenth child unites an
island in an orchestrated ceremony of grief; in *The Candle is
Lighting* the birth of a child in a mountainy farmhouse
galvanises a family and neighbours into a communal ecstasy.
In *The Kings Asleep in the Ground* the recital of ancestral
glories brings a prison warder called O'Brien into guilty
communion with the republican prisoners he is guarding. At
the end of that more recent comic masterpiece, *My Love has
a Long Tail,* the woebegone Mike, who has failed to sell his
greyhound at the Cork Sales, gives public expression to the
suppressed rage of a whole speechless community of the
rural dispossessed:

" 'Peter, you bastard of a spy,' he jerked aloud as if the
other (a jeering neighbour) could hear him, 'I'll best you
yet.' Then turning to address others in an imaginary
audience, 'You too, Hogan, bastard of a big farmer up there
on the hill ready to gobble up my few acres. And you,
bastard of a driver, Tom, that bled me white. Ye bastards at
the track who put me last on the list. You bastard of an
auctioneer and your penciller with the eyes of a fox. Ye
bastards standin' around that gave no bid or that puffed
when is suited. Ye bastards from Amsterdam that never
turned up. You bastards at the traps with your long slip.
You bastard at the store pressing me to pay. Ye bastards in
Brussels who won't let us live. Ye're nothing but a pack of
bastards, the lot of ye. But before the face of Christ I'll beat
ye all yet.' "

This comic version of King Lear in the storm,
persuading us to feel as wretches feel, has its tragic
counterpart in Martin Claffey's outcry at the closed gates of
the honey spike.

In *The World is Lovely and the World is Wide* the same
technical problem arises when an audience of women hidden
behind window curtains hint at a more severe, even

threatening side of communal feeling. A fashionably dressed young woman with 'beauty of calf, buttock and bust' comes into a yard to talk to a man named Danny who is tarring the roof of an outhouse. The two have been lovers, though he now seems to have left her for the woman who is his present employer. They converse in a sort of desperate code, though the meaning of their body language is self-evident to the hidden spectators:

"She came as close as she could without losing sight of him. Face and body were upturned in offering. Her hands made gestures of soft amnesty.

'Danny . . . Danny . . . the two of us together. Look, Danny . . . the world is lovely and the world is wide.' "

But Danny fails to meet the challenge and the woman departs. The women who had been watching make their appearance with "superfluous alabis of brooms and dusters" while their movements "seemed to indicate the communal charge of 'Cheat one, cheat all!' Their lips spat silent imprecations." The narrator must intervene to explain the nature of the women's outrage, the hero's failure, inventing an unspoken monologue in which Danny tries to plead his defeated cause:

"You saw her, didn't you. You were all watching her. Who am I? A man? A man tarring a shed. Or am I then a gannet, nailed to tall air? You saw her, dear women; I know you saw her. She stood there. There! You heard her say 'The world is lovely and the world is wide!' "

In the last sentence it seems to him "that the sun had raised its brass-headed cudgel and clubbed the whole bloody world". The intervention is too overt and there is perhaps too much authorial presence in the story, especially beside the marvellous coded dialogue which is at its centre. These interventions bespeak the difficulty of MacMahon's basic ambition: there is so little scope in the short story form to body forth the feeling of a community. It is basically the difficulty of containing a device of opera within the scope of lyric.

Frank O'Connor in his study of the short story, *The Lonely Voice*, insisted that the short story form is designed to record moments of insight to the lives of lonely individuals amid 'submerged population groups', Chekov's clerks, Maupassant's whores, Lawrence's miners. Like most of his generation O'Connor lamented the breakdown of the organic society of townland, village, island society. His definitive drama of that breakdown is *The Uprooted*; O'Flatherty's is *The Child of God*; O'Faolain's is perhaps *The End of the Record* or more subtly, *The Sugawn Chair*. This obsession provoked Beckett's ridicule when he divided his Irish contemporaries in 'the antiquarians and the others'. It is notwithstanding, of course one of the great modern themes, central to Yeats, Lawrence and Eliot who wrote in 'East Coker'of rural communities:

> . . . . Keeping time
> Keeping the rhythm of their dancing
> As in their living in the living seasons
> The time of the seasons and the constellations
> The time of milking and the time of harvest
> The time of the coupling of man and woman
> And that of beasts. Feet rising and falling.
> Eating and drinking. Dung and death.

MacMahon's archetypal themes. But for Eliot these rhythms have been irreparably broken by the modern world; he looks at them not only as an outsider in time, but in consciousness. His rural folk exist below a certain level of sensibility; their apparent natural bliss depends on their knowing, if not anything better, anything other than their instinctual, seasonal motions. With MacMahon there is no such separation between author and milieu. His project is to expose beneath the routines of his own organic community a liveliness of culture and depth of spiritual consciousness invisible to the crude materialism of the age. In his loyalty to that project he is closer to Daniel Corkery than any other of his precursors. But he exposes himself to far greater risks.

The World is Lovely and the World is Wide, at first or even second glance seems a work of pure realism: the lovers are caught in a moment of vivid revelation; the setting and decor are altogether real; the women, nosey and judgemental, yet life-affirming, are presented convincingly against their quotidian background; their disapproval is understandable, their heart in the right place. Then one becomes aware of the story's deep structure, and all becomes archetypal. These women resent not just the thwarting of romantic love, but more profoundly they hate the rejection of the story's heroine, the flower of the flock, in all her beauty and promise. Danny, the hero, has not only cheated their sex, he has reneged on the tribe. In a profound sense he has sinned against the goddess of fertility. This motley array of females with their mops and dishcloths still keep the mysteries of Spring against the prudential blight of Winter to which Danny has surrendered. So much for the ineluctable archetype.

Yet whether MacMahon likes it or not these vengeful females are, on the level of realism, a little more sinister than he seems to acknowledge. Is there really much room for the independent spirit within that ring of busy-bodies? Could one deconstruct the fable so that it reads as indictment of a society where the really brave ones must leave or suffocate? Is there an unresolved question at the heart of MacMahon's vision – is there a modern satirist quarrelling with the tribal man of ink, a secret *eiron* riding shotgun on the life-affirming *alazon*!* If so is it good or bad for MacMahon's art? I find this question hard to decide.

Is the absence of such ironic questioning from *O, Lonely Moon*! the reason why it is a more satisfying but less intriguing story? There a female conspiracy brings to heel the rambling male, Dublin Jock. When his wife dies giving birth to his tenth child, and he takes to the drink, a powerful old matriarch called Mane – a real priestess of fertiltiy – summons the women of Friary Lane to farm out the children while Jock, a journeyman statue-painter, takes unsteadily to the roads. His last rejected child is bestowed by Mane on Ethel, a sensitive, childless widow the grief of whose barrenness is gestured at in the story's title.

* **Eiron** is Greek for ironic commentator:
* **alazon** for romantic champion.

Towards the climax of the fable, when Jock makes one of his periodic returns, Mane assembles Ethel and the children in Jock's kitchen to contrive a second marriage. At the height of her ritual the children pinion the wanderer and chant 'Marry our father and tie us together!' The wanderer eventually succumbs – he is literally caught in the web. The wounds and dislocations of family and community are healed.

By refusing to waver from its own terms, a comedy of love, fertility and reconcilation, *O, Lonely Moon!* succeeds admirably as a short story. One must go outside these terms if one wants to ask such troubling questions as Jock's right to any say over his children, his fitness as a husband to this vulnerable young woman, Mane's authoritarian contrivances from beginning to end, the ready obedience of child and adult to her commands. The fable triumphs because its conventions prevent the doubts of modernism from penetrating the entrenched culture of Friary Lane, its long-tailed family and traditional life-style.

It is by recourse to these traditional communal values that one accepts the terrible events of *So Early in the Morning O* wherein a mother awakes in the morning and seeks to dissuade her son, the last of her children, from running out on the girl he has got with child:

" 'Be said by me, son! Do the fair thing. Stand your ground here! Easy, Dan! Don't hurt my fingers! There! Why should the woman always handle the dirty end of the stick?' "

The parable with which she seeks to convince him is the story of her own courtship, pregnancy and forced marriage to an arrogant young man whose first caress had been to come down with his ironshod heel on her instep in the course of a dance in the town. In the brutal aftermath of her seduction she becomes a mere chattel as her father and brothers batter and intimidate the reluctant lover into admission of paternity and the promise of marriage. When she runs away and is brought back to face an arranged wedding even her mother proves implacable:

" 'Divine God!' she said. 'Will you bring me disgrace? Think of the others! One wrong, all wrong.'

'I'll not marry him!' "

By tribal assent the troubled pair are left alone together in her kitchen on the night before the marriage, to negotiate their private treaties. They confront each other as enemies until:

"The minute his hand flashed out and tightened on my forearm, I knew that his flesh and mine were pairs. 'Tis only a fooleen of a woman keeps high principles in her head to be made bits of by her limbs.'"

As the mother's narrative concludes they lived happily "until Robber Death came an' took my comrade away". Whether his mother's parable persuades the young man to stand his ground or not, it is clear to the reader that he should. For all its rampant savagery – and MacMahon flinches from none of it – the demands of that society for continuity, and for the mysterious binding force of familial love, seem to override every humane impulse for individual freedom.

So, while MacMahon's fictional world bristles with every form of rebellious human idiocyncrasy, he almost invariably comes down on the side of community, with its family microcosm. In one of his masterpieces, *Exile's Return*, a straightforward story of modern experience, reconciliation is achieved by the instinctive mediation of the child who was to have been the cause of vengeance and estrangement. In *The Gap of Life* the myth of Orpheus and Eurydice stretches across the generations to excite a young couple to an enhanced sense of the sexual mystery. In *The Acolyte* a wound in the community is healed when an errant husband is prevailed upon to use his social position to have his illegitimate son accepted as an altar-boy. When, as in *The Windows of Wonder* a community loses its imaginative vision the legends of a native mythology are called upon to restore it to health.

Yet MacMahon's genius may be at its finest when the tensions and ambiguities of his social world exert their importunities, as in one of his most powerful fictions, *The Broken Lyre*. Here two moralities confront each other with the intimacy of ancient enemies while a well-meaning outsider is destroyed for interfering. Here's the opening paragraph:

"The dark-faced melodian-player, his instrument slung from a strap over his left shoulder, hurried through the town where the cattle fair had long since ended. Stravaging behind him came his red-haired wife, recurrently freeing her fore-arms from the irk of her red-green tartan shawl and shrieking coarse insults at her husband in the savage hope that he would turn and strike her. Farmers standing at the pub doors watched the pair with amusement."

The tinkers and the farmers know each other to the bone. The former, wild, drunken and theatrical, need that stolid, amoral audience to watch as they play out their ritual of love and hate. No move is made to intervene as the man first threatens to kick his instrument to pieces and then proceeds to do so; or when he goes on to beat the woman with an intent and brutal accuracy. It is the half-drunken solider with his alien, simple-minded code of chivalry and fair play who makes the tragic move, taking on the husband in a fist-fight. As he gets the upper hand the tinker's wife strikes him on the head from behind with a stick. When he nevertheless knocks the husband unconscious and thwarts a second attack by the wife she changes tack and begins "to cry out for help in the secret language of the Irish roads."

"The doors of the caravans under the steeple were torn open and the square became suddenly peopled with red-headed men wearing bright plaid shirts. As they meshed out in a quick arc, the ex-soilder's mouth opened in terror of the semi-known."

Finding no allies on the side-walks the ex-soilder takes to his heels out of town and the tinkers set up an epic pursuit.

"This then was the chase: the bloody-polled ex-soilder in front, the running tinkers lumbering after, and the harnessed spring-cart, all silver and bells, moving swiftly behind."

Inexorably the spring cart catches up on the running soldier. When the fugitive realizes that he cannot escape he crouches by the wall and "laces his fingers about his blood-pied poll". The horror of his death is rendered in sickening detail, the driver bringing his cart alongside while his companion prepares his cudgel for the blow: "as the spring-cart hammered past, he drove the heavy knob of his weapon fair through the wicker-work of flesh to crunch audibly on the ex-soldier's skull . . . The broken body keeled and fell ignominiously on its head." As the Guards make their way towards the scene – it is pre-squad-car days – the tinkers drive off furiously into the "open southlands".

In the last movement of the story the lovers who had caused the entire mayhem make their way into the hills where the woman washes her husband's wound, strokes the sore where the melodeon-strap had burned his skin, bites his ear-rim while whispering " 'Me an' you, Mick, an' the world ag'in us', to which her husband assents. In the final tableau "as they stood breast to breast the man and woman were burnished with evening gold".

The story, for all the help we get from MacMahon, seems as empty of moral significance as anything by Issac Babel – and that accounts for much of its power. Yet, at the very core of the fable is the inescapable sense of tribal identity. The tinkers form an outcast population. They beg from, trade with, and prey upon the farmers and shopkeepers who respect them as a breed apart from, if unquestionably beneath, even the lowliest of settled society. On the rural landscape of the Irish southwest, at the time in question, they are tolerated for their colour, theatricality, their occasional usefulness. In a mysterious sense they are envied, because they enact in their uninhibited drinking, violence, and sexuality, some of the fantasies which the settled community barely confess to itself.

The heart of their mystery is therefore in their relationships with themselves, the code by which they live out their freebooting destiny on the edge of conventional society. That, in MacMahon's view, seems to be the source of their endurance, energy and pride. To interfere, to come between them in their more secret affections, is an unpardonable offence, a form of violation. This unspoken, social contract the hapless solider, especially in his half-drunken state, has lost the instinct to perceive. Maybe we are to infer that it has been drilled out of him. The servant of one human code falls tragic victim to the ferocity of another. What more is there to say? This: that Bryan MacMahon is never better than when travelling along these cultural frontiers.

In concentrating on the archetypal patterns at the heart of Bryan MacMahon's fiction I naturally take as read his matchless skill as a storyteller, the lyrical energy of his prose style, his mastery of dialogue, his subtle and varied narrative technique, the individuality with which he imbues even the most minor of his characters, his uncanny sense of place, his ability to create a world within the compass of his shortest fiction. When, after thirty years as his reader, I accepted the invitation – and the challenge – to write about him, the theme and emphasis literally chose me. There are many other aspects of his work to be explored, but this is the focus and lode-stone of my personal fascination. He has himself described analytical criticism as 'slitting the sky-lark's throat to find the secret of its song'. In a sense I'm relieved that I've left so much of his secret intact, having barely ruffled the neck feathers.

BEING SAID: TEXT AND CONTEXT IN THE WORK OF JOHN B. KEANE
BY RICHARD PINE

This lecture discusses the work of John B. Keane in three ways: firstly, by suggesting why he deserves thorough critical attention, and by asking why he has not yet received that attention; secondly, by discussing the importance of what he has to say, and why his plays of twenty-five years ago continue to command a position on the Irish and international stage; and thirdly, by commenting on the difference between what Keane says in the play *The Field* and what is said in the film of the same title. It addresses these ideas in terms of recent productions of four of Keane's plays: *Sive, The Field, Big Maggie* and *The Year of the Hiker*.[1]

* * * *

John B. Keane has until very recently been neglected by critics because his manner does not easily lend itself to critical analysis. Where his most significant living contemporaries, Brian Friel and Tom Murphy, have received full-length critical assessment,[2] commentaries on Keane's work have been limited to a few quasi-academic articles and pieces for journals.[3] The tone of those commentaries has largely been a mixture of condescension and embarrassment, the result of not knowing quite how to approach the idea of folk drama or how to accommodate a discussion of it within the mainstream of Irish dramatic criticism.

---

[1] All page references in the text refer to the revised scripts of *Sive, The Field* and *Big Maggie* published by Mercier Press, Cork, in 1990.

[2] see particularly: Richard Pine, *Brian Friel and Ireland's Drama,* London & New York, Routledge, 1990; Fintan O'Toole, *The Politics of Magic: The Work and Times of Tom Murphy,* Dublin, Raven Arts Press, 1987.

[3] see Anthony Roche, interview with John B. Keane in *Theatre Ireland* no. 18, April-June 1989; Richard Pine, 'Rough Edges:Commitment in Contemporary Irish Drama,' Dublin, Arts Ireland, 1989.

Furthermore, there is a significant difference between the way Keane speaks and the way Friel, Murphy or even Frank McGuinness (the contemporary playwright with whom Keane has most in common) talk about themselves and their work. It is customary for Irish playwrights to talk obliquely; they speak not in the language of their plays but in a kind of subtext, putting a gloss on the work, helping the critic, in language and terms they have agreed to adopt for the purpose. But Keane speaks directly, using the language of his plays. As I shall have cause to underline later, he can talk as Bull McCabe or Big Maggie talk, seeing the world through their eyes, not a playwright's eyes. Where the language of Friel and Murphy is consciously well-crafted, making the English language part of Irish dramatic speech, Keane's remains resolutely Irish, translating an older way of seeing.

However, I do not accept that there is a qualitative difference between Keane's drama and Friel's or Murphy's: in any case, the laid-back, restrained cogency of Friel's later plays is unlike anything in Murphy's apocalyptic writing, and is equally far removed from the urgent pleading of McGuinness or the frenetic agony of Tom MacIntyre or Michael Harding.

The only way that a case can be made for treating Keane separately is by insisting on his naïveté: he does not attempt to write sophisticated plays, he does not aspire to high art. But the very compelling productions of *Sive*, *The Field*, *Big Maggie* and *The Year of the Hiker*, directed in recent years by Ben Barnes (mostly at the National Theatre[1]) have led to a feeling that their author should be 'reconsidered' – especially in relation to the theatre which originally rejected him in 1959.[2]

---

[1] *Sive* was revived at the Abbey Theatre in 1985; *The Field* in 1987; *Big Maggie* in 1988. *The Year of the Hiker* was revived at the Gaiety Theatre, Dublin, 1990.

[2] *Sive* was offered to the Abbey Theatre in 1958, and rejected by its then Chairman, Ernest Blythe. Premiered by the Listowel Amateur Drama Group in 1959, it went on to win the overall Irish amateur

Certainly, Keane's plays are naïve: the only modern Irish plays with which they bear extended comparison are those of Synge and Fitzmaurice, and there are strong reasons for making distinctions between all three writers: Keane's plays are much simpler in plot, much less ambitious, more pointed, than Synge's, and much less difficult to apprehend than Fitzmaurice's, although all three writers belong to a folk theatre, if not a folk tradition. The language of each is quite different, invented for separate purposes. Keane puts much less effort into this process, because he writes as he talks, directly, not out of imagination but out of knowledge of how and what the world is. Somehow, drama critics find this difficult to take. And this is in fact Keane's distinctive achievement, and his major problem with those critics, because he succeeds in puzzling and alienating the minds of those who might otherwise explore that world of his.

Sive is a crude play – especially the suicide, which is a forgivable and predictable fault in a first play – but its crudity in fact supplies a powerful metaphor for the violence at the heart of the play: the bartering of the bride is symbolic of the gap in human experience, in humankindness, which the matchmaker fills, in his own words, by *making love between people (p. 17)*. These are not dramas: they are melodramas, spectacles in which the music – both the music sung and the music inherent in the text – creates a kind of opera in which the actual incidents we witness are less important than the emotional experience that the writer intends us to feel. I shall have more to say about this later.

If we think of the difference between what a play is *about* and the playwright's *intention*, we will see why Keane's plays are much easier to apprehend than much contemporary Irish dramas, but at the same time more difficult to talk about in the same terms. *Hamlet* is 'about' a young man's distraction at the murder of his father, a young girl's distraction at her lover's madness. But that is not what Shakespeare intended us to concentrate on: these are merely the backdrop to a discussion of the nature of madness and

---

drama award of the year and, under these auspices, found its way to the Abbey stage (at the Queen's Theatre).

conscience. Similarly, in *The Field*, the sale of a piece of land and the murder of an outsider are not the end of the play: they are a means of discussing the nature of hunger. In *Big Maggie* the way the widow celebrates her new freedom covers the subtext about her 'hardness of concern', and the silence of her impossible lust. In *The Year of the Hiker* the homecoming, important though it is, is a way of highlighting the question of freedom and wanderlust.

Sive is crude, but the re-introduction of melodrama into Irish theatre which Keane achieved with that play was a stroke of genius: a Greek chorus consisting of two tinkers will lend credibility to the most loutish and commonplace of tricks, and credibility is what Keane badly needs, in order to make those tricks work. The tricks are there to divert attention from the way he builds up a dramatic fiction into a truth that we are prepared to take home at the end of the evening and try out in our own lives, to measure against our own experience.

This is very committed drama, and although little critical attention was paid to Keane's plays before the revival of *Sive* at the Abbey Theatre in 1985, they did have their effect: Friel's *Faith Healer*, for example, with its conscientious exploration of the nature of freedom, owes much to the spirit, if not the letter, of *The Year of the Hiker*.

But there are also huge differences. There are few memorable passages in Keane's plays, fewer focal points than we find in plays by Friel and Murphy, and conversely a much greater sense of violence and concentrated hurt when they do occur. It is interesting to note that the only play by Friel which exhibits the same overt indignation and sorrow as a Keane play is *The Freedom of the City*, where he makes a direct attempt to confront the incidents of Bloody Sunday. Keane confronts similar events, but largely private events, in all these plays, and the result is often brutal. In a play like *The Field* he makes the same attempt as Friel, uniting a public event to a private conscience, and in doing so he links his community to itself.

So the difference which seems to have affected his critics lies in Keane's 'aboutness' rather than in his intentions, in the way we have allowed the simplicity of what happens on stage to obscure the nature and force of what he is really saying. In joining Friel and Murphy and McGuinness in a retreat from the public world, he is part of the current of contemporary drama. He deserves the same treatment as they receive because he is asking the same questions. The dramatic impact is, ultimately, the same, because whether we carry the message away in the forefront of the brain or somewhere in the subconscious, the effect is to make us reflect on the nature of change, on the nature of sexuality, on the nature of conscience, all of which are compelling questions for Irish society. Keane unites the shape of the world to the shape of the play, because he doesn't actually care about the shape of the play. It takes its form from the knowledge he has about the world: in Fitzmaurice's words, his world is populated by the 'wicked old children'[1] of North Kerry whom we find throughout the world.

*   *   *   *

Why then do plays written thirty years ago continue to resonate within the Irish experience?

Let me answer that question by means of a short history lesson: in 1847, in a funeral oration for Daniel O'Connell in Rome, warning was given of 'the revolution which threatens to encompass the globe'[2]. It is ironic that the changes to which O'Connell contributed largely passed Ireland by. Catholic Emancipation was not Irish emancipation. It deliverd the majority of Irish people from one form of colonisation into another. The intellectual emancipation of the Irish mind, from the condition of poverty and the culture of failure, the conquest of displacement and wishful thinking, never took place. That culture stands behind every

---

[1] Fitzmaurice's description of the folk in his plays is quoted in Austin Clarke, introduction to *The Plays of George Fitzmaurice: Vol. 1: Dramatic Fantasies*, Dolmen Press, 1972, p. viii.

[2] Father Joachim Ventura, quoted in L.B. Namier, *1848: The Revolution of the Intellectuals*, London, British Academy, 1946, p.3.

word and gesture of Bull McCabe's passionate, raging hunger for land and behind every nuance of Big Maggie's sexual imprisonment.

Paradoxically, therefore, although the Irish mind is superbly placed to diagnose the problems of the colonised, it is no fit state to initiate the solution. 'Physician, heal thyself' is a motto that does not run here. The economic and social changes we have seen in the past century have not been matched in the intellectual sphere. Modern Ireland continues to chase one goal – a place among the nations of the world – while actually embracing another: the continued condition of being colonised by the clientelist mentality.

There is thus a dichotomy between the aspiration to individual or collective liberty and actually achieving that liberty. Ireland offers – and has been offering since at least the close of the eighteenth century – a textbook example of how to imagine a possible future while living with the memory of an impossible past. Whereas we witness today a growing awareness of the failure of the European imagination, Ireland has no such failure because the Irish mind has always been at home with the notion of imaginary failure.

We have to couple this long history of depression with the fact that in the pagan, peasant culture which has been only superficially overlaid by bourgeois pretensions, the chief motives for action have been, and continue to be, a love-hate relationship with the land and a paranoiac individualism. These two factors make it difficult on the one hand to address any topic which interferes with that love-hate relationship; on the other, to bring Irish men and women to look communally at any issue. Rape – which is the murder of sexuality – or any other kind of death, any form of commerce between the sexes, any restructuring of the social orders, is conceived in images relating to the land and the individual's struggle for meaning in terms of the land:

In the name of God, what do the likes of us know about love? Did you ever hear the word of love on his lips? Did he ever give you a little rub behind the ear or run his fingers through your hair and tell you that he would swim the Shannon for you? Did he ever sing the love-songs for you in the far-out part of the night when ye do be alone? He would sooner to stick his snout in a plate of mate and cabbage or to rub the back of a fattening pig than whisper a bit of his fondness for you (*Sive* p. 37) –

words which find their way thirty years later into Michael Harding's play *Una Pooka*, set against the Pope's visit to Ireland.[1]

Terms of endearment are reserved for the land; tremors of emotion are caused by the health and welfare of the land or the policemen of the Catholic conscience, not by the tenderness of that most under-used word in the Irish lexicon – love. The history lesson ends with the observation that people who have been traumatised, wounded in their psyche and their sex, have longer memories, more acute memories, than those whose days have been filled with hazy laughter and sunshine. The journey inward makes cowards of us all, and Keane's rallying cry is to defeat that cowardice.

If one Kerryman, O'Connell, initiated change, another reacts to it. Keane laments the death of loyalty, of courtesy, respect and regard for others, especially for the old, the simple and the vulnerable. He is impeded as a playwright by the fragmentation of society, the growth of ruthlessness, of needless violence, by the lack of conscience. The man who created Bull McCabe in 1965 would find it hard to recreate him today, and the problem has contributed significantly to Keane's recent silence as a playwright. Ironically, if there had been censorship of the stage, Keane's work would probably have suffered the same fate as John McGahern's: it is unlikely that *Big Maggie* would have survived as a novel in the 1960s and drama critics would do well to examine this. Yet the problem remains the same: how does an individual succeed in singing his own song? And how does

---

[1] Michael Harding, *Una Pooka*: the line, from the typescript, is: 'You need a man who will love you with all the razzmatazz of his body. He would feel the flank of a prize heifer sooner than he'd feel you'.

a nation achieve the right to self-determination? The way Keane has asked these questions is a parable of modern Irish nationalism set against the twin empires of British colonialism and Catholic authority.

If there is a national story, it is the repatriation, the rehabilitation, of the *amadán*, the liar, the wanderer and the deviant. Synge suggests it in the heroic failure of Christy Mahon, Yeats in the Cuchulainn cycle, and it has been central to the work of John B. Keane. Keane is the archetypal playwright for modern Ireland because Mike Glavin, Bull McCabe, Hiker Lacy and their kind are the central characters of a drama still being played out in the towns and villages of Ireland. City life has covered it with a bourgeois layer of respectability. But the 'real Ireland' continues to excel in the eloquence of the stuttering lover. The paradox of that drama is that a society and its civilisation may contain dreamers, liars, poets, cowards, but that dreamers, liars, poets and cowards cannot contain a civilisation. The outsider, the deviant, the rebel, the wanderer, are central rather than peripheral to the Irish experience.

If that condition is highlighted by a dramatic experience, as it is in these four plays of Keane, our awareness of that condition stops being subconscious and becomes a painfully articulated fact. The liars whom we find in Friel's *Faith Healer, Living Quarters, Making History* or Murphy's *Bailegangaire, The Gigli Concert, Too late For Logic*, McGuinness's *The Bread Man*, like Keane's witnesses, all descend from Synge's Christy Mahon. The solitary exception might be Big Maggie herself, but I will discuss that point later.

The central motive of Irish drama therefore becomes an attempted homecoming. In many ways Keane expresses this more successfully than the others precisely because, like O'Casey, he is so direct, so unequivocal. When he makes political statements, we are left in no doubt. Lack of subtlety will never disqualify a playwright from the heights of distinction, unless the critics who award the accolades are blinkered and closeted by bourgeois values inimical to the roots of drama.

Homecoming is of course the paramount object of human longing, the central ambition of the folk-tale from which all drama derives. Greek drama – think of *Oedipus Rex* or *Medea* or *Antigone* – gets on with telling a story. The events of Greek drama – its 'aboutness' – may be wrapped up in philosophy, but they are not packaged in hypocrisy or prejudice. If there is rhetoric, it is, in the original sense, public speaking which encompasses the private conversation. Similarly, Bull McCabe's outburst –

There's a law for them that's priests and doctors and lawmen. But there's no law for us – (*p. 166*)

is a neat polarisation of the issues prevalent in a society that continues to practice double standards in its clientelist political system. When Bull remonstates –

I'll ask God questions. There's a lot of questions I'd like to ask God. Why does God put so much misfortune in the world? Why does God make me one way and you another? (*p. 166*) –

he speaks with the same tongue of the wounded, the outcast, the deviant which drama has given them since drama began. The mission of the rebel is to tell the truth as he sees it, however unpalatable it may be. The mission of the playwright is to make it credible and compelling for his audience.

Keane's commitment to his mission is equally obvious: there are times not only when he speaks with the words of Bull McCabe and Big Maggie but when he *becomes*[1] Bull or Maggie themselves, so passionate is his identification with the sinner.

The criteria of homecoming and of singing one's own song are rigorous: a society, like a traveller on a winter's night, must be able

---

[1] see Anthony Roche, interview in *Theatre Ireland* already referred to.

– to find the right road home
– to cross the threshold
– to announce its arrival
– to take its place at the hearth
– to have something significant to say
– to demonstrate its capacity for saying it.

A predominantly visionary culture – one that thinks in an imagistic language – will have the added burden of articulating that vision. When Big Maggie states

> there's enough lies written on the headstones of Ireland without my adding to them (*p. 175*)

she creates a powerful metaphor for precisely that purpose. When Bull McCabe binds his community together in the central lie of *The Field* he achieves the same effect:

> When the civic guards come with their long noses all of you will remember that Tadhg and myself were in this pub at the time (*p. 136*).

When he goes on to add

> twill be the same as if we never left (*p. 137*)

we realise the full force of what he is doing because in using the 'as if' of a visionary culture he is creating the lie *before* the murder and validating it *after*. During the night scene on the road the people of Carraigthomond remain in suspended animation in Mick Flanagan's pub. Bull thereby succeeds in creating an unnatural story that everyone knows but no-one can tell.

The keynote of this drama is *embarrassment* – the gap at the centre of every human transaction. Where there is no love, Thomasheen must make love between people. Where there is no understanding, Bull must fill the gap with brutality. The central experience in each of these plays is that of emptiness, of a promise unfulfilled, and they

challenge the national dream which insists that Ireland is free
and at peace.

Think of the situation in *Sive*: if there were no
embarrassment in that society, the cursing songs of Pats
Bocock and Carthalawn would have no meaning, no grip on
reality. But palpably they do have meaning because they
frighten and disorientate. Some are prepared to
acknowledge that – Nanna says 'there was always a
welcome here for Pats Bocock' (*p. 48*) – whereas others,
those concerned for respectability, reject it out of fear and
insecurity. And not only the characters on stage, but their
audience: we may go to *Sive* expecting to be mildly
entertained, but we leave knowing something more about
ourselves. If one is truly powerful, in touch with the roots
of one's psyche, one can hold a cursing song in the hollow
of one's hand. If one is weak, unsure of one's true
condition, it will destroy you, whatever century and
civilisation you belong to.

*   *   *   *

Which brings me to my title, and the centre of my argument.

In that splendidly bleak play, *Sive*, Mena is fighting
desperately for respectability by marrying the orphan, Sive,
to Sean Dota. Although he is a crawling *amadán*, Mike
Glavin is hesitant, conscious of his responsibility towards
the child. Mena silences him with the single brutal, explicit,
devasting line:

will you sit down and be said by me (*p. 27*)

To be said – to have no song of one's own but only to be a
part of someone else's superior narrative – is to be
colonised, a victim of history, dominated by myth.

　Being said is the lowest of roles. Big Maggie's marriage
was a symbol of the women of Ireland being said by their
husbands, their fathers and their church. Bull McCabe is the
symbol of the continuing war between landlord and tenant.
The landlord, whether church or state, owns the *amadán*.
The song sings the singer, because he is not in command of

his own mind. As Hiker Lacy tells us, every man has one song. It's all he needs. Hiker Lacy is not thrown out, he submits to no-one else's narrative. He steps out of the house for a minute that lasts twenty years, and he steps back in again.

When someone is said, they are written out of the text, and become merely the context for someone else's actions and speech. To regain their life, they have to do something catastrophic: Sive must fall into the bog; Bull must kill William Dee; Maggie and the Hiker must systematically destroy their homes, because they were never homes. They have to destroy life, faith and the integrity of the family, in order to reconstitute it.

But by so doing they recreate not only themselves but their community which they carry within them. By means of suicide, murder, disease and coldheartedness they grant a form of redemption, a transformative experience, to their own folk. This is why the plays of Keane are so powerful, because they underline the fact that this age of ours remains a time of folk, still searching for the moral autonomy without which we cannot get on with living.

The tramps and the downtrodden in these plays have a special language: we must continually remind ourselves that we are in the presence of an imagination that refuses to be strait-jacketed into always logical thought or modes of expression. When Bull welds his community into that central surrealist lie he creates an image with all the vehemence and rhythm of Carthalawn's songs. There is, as in the plays of Fitzmaurice, an inevitable confusion between the familiar and the bizarre, between the real and fantastic, and it becomes something which priest and policeman cannot come to terms with, because it is created out of despair and rage which belong to a different order.

Words take on new burdens. Outsiders recognise them, but they cannot truly know them. And there is a point in these plays where we, the audience, are convinced that the central character is in command of all the words. The point of acquiescing in someone else's narrative is that the rest of the community accepts that person as their natural focus and thereafter stands in crucial relation to him or her. Thereafter their role is to hear history being made, and to sing that song. Their dream becomes the conventional image of the future.

But what does this do to us? We are left with a society waiting for miracles. It is a very bleak prospect: the playwright takes a great risk in putting such huge burdens on the shoulders of his heroes. To do so, he must make those shoulders structurally broad enough to carry the weight of their language and their gestures, and therein lies the fusion of form and content. There is no room for the play to have its own form, because the central character fills it by exploring the emptiness of the human heart.

The moment of metamorphosis, when an individual changes the nature of a whole society, makes it see the vision, persuades it of his truth, is a moment that fills the whole world. Since this transformative experience begins with the collision of the known and the impossible, of fact and dream, this is a risk that sometimes brings a play to the edge of absurdity. When strange, estranged people come together out of a landscape instinct with semen and blood, into a community of hurt, seeking redemption, they will inevitably surprise, offend and alienate the spectator, especially when the texture and fabric of that landscape – country lane, bar grocery, cottage, graveyard – is so ordinary and so familiar. The stage disappears. We are bound to feel uncomfortable. Saints and criminals co-exist because they are part of the music that connects nature with the dream life. It is intensely political, because it confronts reality with an alternative vision, a different way of seeing and saying the world. It invests the public occasion with all its pretence, and the private continuity with all its hurts and joys. It suggests beauty, it hints at the play of life, but primarily it transfers wisdom to the audience because we partake of those visions and those truths.

Keane's plays are therefore necessarily restricted. Where Synge's plays remain the outsider's view of the west, Keane's are North Kerry's view of North Kerry. But in another sense they go much further. They are North Kerry's view of the wide world. Bull McCabe encompasses the

108

whole of creation in asking questions of God; Hiker Lacy has been there to see it for himself.

For this reason melodrama is perfectly suited to the theatre where form is subordinate to content, plot to spectacle. At the turning point, we see that the lie is in life itself, the absurdity of what we do every day. All plot is absurd, because plot is fate.

Keane's relevance as a playwright therefore rests on two points: firstly, on his resolute forthright way of saying things; secondly, on the local nature of his language and settings.

I would like to underline this by reflecting for a moment on how he handles the issue of emptiness, which becomes the focal point of each of these plays, sometimes early on, sometimes much later.

Let us remember that the Latin word *focus* literally means the *hearth*. These are plays where the writer creates a focal point, an imaginary hearth, because they have no true hearth.

Of course in each play – except *The Field* – we are admitted to the privacy of a space which has the semblance of a home, but the controlling emotion is that of absence: the true emotional pitch is found in *The Field*, where the community focus or hearth is the public place of the bar and the open road, where the living space which is the emptiness and loneliness of Bull's marriage is described but not seen. (I will say something about the film of *The Field* in this regard at a later stage.) In the same way, Hiker Lacy only makes sense when he talks of the life of the vagabond, the homelessness of his imagination, his freedom.

Therefore we are never at home in these plays unless we are first outlawed, pushed out of our material and emotional assumptions. The spectacle of Mena Glavin is not a pretty sight: the violent fury of the barren woman, caged like a wounded lioness inside her own fruitlessness, craving the meaning of home, within a house that will never be a home, will never again know the laughter and tears of children.

We are back in the jungle, in the world where marriage is 'a fight to the death.' The place of the struggle is the kitchen. The time of the struggle is now, at the end of the world.[1] The chief characters are always the same: they are the conditions of life, the factors that make men and women hungry, mad, rotten and poor: the fear of emptiness, of loneliness. The accusation, to borrow a line from Frank McGuinness's *The Bread Man* is: "you stole my life." Bull carries within him images of what home and life should be, knowing that they can never be. He sees a threshold leading to a hearth, and he knows that if he can find the way and sing the right song he can take his seat at the hearth and become a whole man.

Life in these plays becomes a Punch and Judy show, not least because they derive their imaginative power and emotional force from the same source: the European folk dramas which became the *commedia dell'arte* of the seventeenth century: a combination of circus pantomime and opera which embraces all the stock situations of life. The scraggy beard, the cod-piece, the intercepted letter, the poisoned cup, continue to characterise the European imagination, satisfying its prurient curiosity for other people's misfortunes. Ballads remain the newsletter which broadcasts the loves and murders of town and mountain.

There is little room for subtlety precisely because, in the presence of the emotional forces evoked – fear, love, lust, greed, pretence, hatred – we have little time for sophistication. So much psychic energy is burned up in the presence of the archetypal figures drawn up out of our subconscious that it is all we can do to tolerate their impact.

In an age which is worried by content, form tends to predominate. And this is an age which fears content – fears the naked expression of deeply-known truths and suspicions which might disturb the tranquillity of conscience. Keane's plays have a pagan ferocity and disregard for city life that challenge the state-ridden, church-ridden mentality of contemporary Ireland. His drama is radical in the sense that

---

[1] 'The time of the struggle is now, at the end of the world'. I have consciously paraphrased the stage direction for the setting of Michael Harding's *Strawboys*: The action takes place at the end of the world, at the time of the last argument'.

it concentrates on the roots of experience, not just the upper branches.

It is, in fact, in the skilful stylisation and presentation of the stock characters and in the provision of blunt speech which gives no space to nicety, that Keane succeeds in catching our conscience. We are brought face to face with the fact that the function of language is not principally the creation of beauty or the expression of pleasantries, but the way of expressing a view of the world. It may of course be the occasion of beauty, or of ugliness, but that is not its function: ultimately, language is the means whereby we discover our differences about the world.

When a character passes the time of day in a Keane play, we know he means something else. Language defines the characters because they are never given inferior or purposeless lines. They are in one sense strait-jacketed, spancelled by their lines, because we now know them for what they are: liar, pimp, *amadán*, bully, tramp, mother, bastard. But they are also liberated by the same lines, because they bring with them the freedom to explore the role in which Keane has cast them. Every nuance will tell a story.

It is not only in the gestures and obscenities, the crude stylisations or blunt speech that Keane highlights these stereotypes. In the sidelines, the oblique side of speech, he creates horrid portraits of the commerce between town and mountain. When the go-between tells Mike Glavin

> there was a great housekeeper lost in you. You have the gameze and the antics of a woman the way you handle the brush (*p. 71*)

he condemns him to the misery of a halfway house, fit only to be parodied, to be said. In this way Keane eliminates the characters who lend nothing to the drama, leaving those who have strong words, a clear song however horrid its message and its vision may be.

*   *   *   *

This, unfortunately, is what the film of *The Field* lacks. The film has if anything served to obscure rather than enhance Keane's stature because it succumbs to the colonist's view of Ireland as an ideological failure that feeds off its own image of itself as a green and pleasant land still fighting the land war and living off lost dreams. Its imagery is clientelist, encouraging the poor mouth rather than the raging rebel. Bull becomes an apology for life rather than a reason for living, and this is nowhere more severely underlined than in borrowing the landscape of Connemara rather than using Stack's Mountains, and in painting the field itself greener than any emerald, real or imagined.

It is a monstrous rewrite of the original text, in which the song is lost. It diverts attention away from Bull in the community to give a pathetic series of insights into Bull at home. The emptiness of home, as Bull describes it, as he and Tadhg wait on the road for William Dee, is forfeited in the cinema for a series of complicated ancedotes about the nature of embarrassment, based on Bull's conscience and his conversations with God.

We do not need the wife, the invented elder son, the tinkers, Tadhg's badgering of the widow, Dee's complicity with the priest, to convince us of the gravity of the situation. That gravity is diffused by the piling of scene on scene which play down Bull's power and play up the greatness of poverty.

There is no focal point and therefore no moment of transformation from that poverty into identity, no welding together of the elements, no carrying of the community across the bridge from doubt to certainty. It fails in this because it has no original concept to be faithful to: it doesn't matter if it loses faith with Keane's text, because its obvious, and quite honest, intention is to deliver part of Ireland to Hollywood. Hence Richard Harris rather than Niall Toibín.

The best that can be said about the film is that it is loosely based on an idea by John B. Keane, with a new plot by Jim Sheridan, and additional cinematic inspiration supplied by *Man of Aran, The Quiet Man, Ryan's Daughter* and *December Bride,* with apologies to *The Playboy of the*

Western World, Darby O'Gill and the Little People and *Far From the Madding Crowd.*

Let us not be too unfair: the film tells a narrative superbly well, but a false narrative. In the play, Keane strives to convince us that Bull's truth, however macabre and however battered it may be, can be our truth, that we can derive strength from his song. The film, by denying him the song, by making him beg before the priest rather than assert the truth of his vision, diminishes his strength, narrowing rather than broadening his shoulders. It cares too much for 'aboutness', for a storyline that over-describes the scenery, the land that is the reason for the emptiness and the longing. Ironically, the film continues to persuade us that we are on a film set, insisting on the theatricality of the view, the rhetorical bogland that comes between the viewer and its own story. Form triumphs over content, as if each frame were of greater importance than the overall picture that was in the original viewfinder.

*   *   *   *

Finally, I come back to the question of whether Maggie Polpin is different from the other liars in Keane's plays. The answer highlights both the dramatic strengths and pitfalls. The weakness consists in the way he often waits until the last possible moment before creating the miracle that saves the play and the community of interest. His rewriting of the end of *Big Maggie* makes the miracle clearer, but it is still very much nearer to the twelfth hour than the eleventh.

Certainly Maggie is a good liar. We see her using a mixture of truth and lies to destroy her household as ruthlessly as Hiker Lacy, and provoking her community as viciously as Bull McCabe. But she does not leave home herself, and she creates no opportunity for homecoming for her children. Or does she? She does leave home herself in her imagination, continually taking that long walk into her inner place where she meets Martin the cowman.

But what kind of hearth is she building? What focal point is she drawing us towards in that fine, simple line

I'm alone now but I'm free, and not too many women can say that (*p. 234*)?

Who is she bringing with her in her reverie? It would be no use if her sole companions were *mná na hÉireann*: she must emancipate all of the Irish men, too, or the gesture is insufficient.

Maybe the focal point is simply that brief moment of recognition, the unfulfilled second between herself and Martin. Maybe the hearth is only imagined, something that flits in and out of existence as, in her dream, she takes possession of her sex and of the man she fancies. She shows us how to turn the bitterness of a desperate woman like Mena Glavin into strength and power. But she does so at huge cost, by crushing the spirit of her daughters.

The pivotal moment of the play is not the way she deals with her frightened sons, but the torturing of her wayward daughter. The reason? Because that daughter is too much like the dead father who could never keep his hands to himself. Maggie Polpin in fact acts like a man in redressing the wound to her sex. It's a terrible scene, the mother roaring 'have I raised a whore?' (*p. 199*) and the daughter being forced to admit 'I was committing a sin with him' (*p. 199*).

Maggie's common ground with Bull and Hiker is in her hurt and her refusal. She makes the inward journey alone, in violence and in grief and in outrage, denying herself every outward detail of life except her memory – a roadside vision trying to outweigh the imprisonment of marriage, family and confessional.

So the importance of *Big Maggie* in the range of these four plays is that it pushes to even more painful limits the fact that moral autonomy includes the need for lying. The lie is told in the barren years of marriage when she lusted silently after the cowman. This lie is made true in her closing speech when she makes herself available to any man if he fancies her and she fancies him. Whether she finds, in her own wonderful words, 'a man brimming with sap and taspy, a man who'll be a a real match for Big Maggie Polpin' (*p. 235*) is not important. John B. Keane is one of the few

Irishmen capable of using the words 'I love', and the tremendously important thing is that it gives him the capacity to take the woman's part, whether it's Mena Glavin's misery or Maggie Polpin's triumph. It gives her her emancipation from the rape, the murder, of the marriage bed, and thereby it frees the whole of Ireland.

"SINGING TO ME OF WHO AND WHY I AM"
BRENDAN KENNELLY'S JUDASCAPE
BY MARK PATRICK HEDERMAN

And I thought how poets wage a spiritual battle
To shed some light on the unprofitable mess,
Blessing what others curse, cursing what others
bless.

The Book of Judas combines a labour of Hercules with a
forgotten book of The New Testament in one volume. On
the cover, the B of Brendan and the K of Book intertwine to
form a frame around Giotto's famous Judaskiss, the fresco
of betrayal. The poem tries to explain this kiss and the "poor
fucker" who delivered it. The 'labour' involves an
excavation of all sides of the picture. Just as Adam has been
nominated father and representative of the human race and
Christ depicted theologically as its mystical body, so, too,
Judas is Everyman and, *a fortiori*, every Irish person, both
of whom feature prominently and without much distinction
in the text.

Evacuating a space for Judas in the Irish psyche and
rehabilitating the scapegoat who has been the convenient peg
for all our treacherous hangups is a herculean task. The poet
divides the labour between twelve books, which in itself is a
suggestive number: The twelve labours of Hercules, the
Twelve tribes of Israel, meant to represent the chosen race,
and the Twelve apostles chosen to replace them and
supposedly the contrary opposite of the last of their number
who was later eradicated. The particular labour of Hercules
which seems to cover a similar area would be the famous
'cleansing of the cattle stables of King Augeus', where the
herd included 'twelve white bulls sacred to his father' and
the mess was only horrendous! The Encyclopaedia
Brittanica describes Hercules as "an enormously strong man
of moderate height; a huge eater and drinker, very amorous,
generally kindly but with occasional outbursts of brutal

rage." The cleaner of this poetic version describes himself and the "Jobs" in hand:[1] (43-44)

> . . . At nineteen I started to drink
> Porter Phoenix Carlsberg Smithwicks Power Jameson
>
> Anything then. Then I stopped it,
> Got a job in the sewers. With
> Helmet gloves rubber clothes flashlamp
> I went down below Dublin
>
> From Kingsbridge into O'Connell Street,
> Flashin' me lamp in the eyes o' rats
> Diabolical as tomcats. Rats don't like light
> In their eyes.

In the preface (p. 9) the poet explains why the job is so specifically necessary in Ireland:

> There is something in Irish life which demands that you over-simplify practically everything. This is another way of saying that everybody must be labelled, made readily accessible, explainable.

Christianity in Ireland, and Kennelly believes 'that the culture of these islands is, broadly speaking, Christian', has developed into such a simplified version of the original mystery that 'this culture is now in an advanced state of self-parody. Or, if you wish, in an advanced state of self-betrayal, playing Judas to itself.'

The oversimplification is partly the refusal to admit the necessity of exploring our underground sewer. Christian hypocrisy in this regard is a betrayal of essential humanity. Are we not, as Judas possibly was, 'a shrewd refuser of what might have made him loveable and vulnerable?' (11) The fearful obstruction of an essential part of our make-up,

---

[1] All page references are to *The Book of Judas*, A Poem by Brendan Kennelly, Bloodaxe Books, 1991.

caused by an oversimplified and sterilized version of same and the banishment of what is rejected to a hidden gloom of maligned and repudiated shadows, inevitably creates a lawless untrammelled underworld where parts of us live on in dangerously schizophrenic isolation. Kennelly sets himself the task in this poem of giving tongue to this Judasphere. He follows the 'Judasvoice as it appeared in words before his eyes.' He found it 'odd and ordinary, freakish and free, severed and pertinent ' (10) as will anyone who reads the book. However, it would be a mistake to imagine that *The Book of Judas* is about anyone but ourselves. 'To what extent', Kennelly wonders in an interview about his work[1], 'have we elected Judas to be our real redeemer from the consequences of what we have ourselves created but like to blame somebody else for, when things go wrong?'

And so we are taken through twelve books giving voice to the smothered Judas. Stop talking about it "Do it" the first part tells us. The difficulty is that "Judas is the shrewdest whore/ That ever stacked a man with a galloping disease"(19). All this poetry could be Judashit as easily as Judasense.

> The scene splattered apart in rags and tatters
> Epic story? Whimpering scene? Which matters?

The first part 'Do it', under the aegis of that first actionman apostle Peter: 'But Peter always did what Peter had to do/In this we are not unalike'. (20), still leaves open the question of part two: 'Are the poems honest, doctor?' or are they just another way of reinforcing the myth:

> Let my story feed the children
> Who need a monster to hate and fear.(47)

The poet is still aware of the difficulties and dangers of his task:

---

[1] Interview with Katie Donovan, *Irish Times*, 19 December 1991.

Even if I said what I have to say
It'd be a lie in the end, long before the end,
One word after another, tale, song, poem, lie;

I must operate on myself, the question is how.(45)

By the time we reach part three we all "hear the pages crying" and "the book seemed to write itself "(60) about a world of adulterers, childmolesters, informers, pimps, racists, spies, terrorists. But, maybe "no image fits" (53) and maybe:

My book stinks of sickness, a sweaty sense of
   dying
Into the notion that truth becomes helpless
   lying.(61)

So that what the poet is creating is a "heady odyssey in non-existence" or, as he calls part four, "bunk". The truth may be that the search for a Judasvoice is a false trail because 'you have no voice I recognize as yours/ Unless it be this laneway packed with shadows, hungers.'

Open your hearts to the Holy Spirit
For Christ's sake.
We'll be back to you in a moment
After this commercial break. (68)

The real commercial break comes in part seven called 'High on Silver'. If we follow the catechism order of the twelve apostles we find that Matthew, the tax collector, holds this position and we are into the notorious area of the bribe, 'the stock exchange', jewels, coins, money bags and the infamous thirty pieces of silver laid out in a poem a piece.
   Then 'one liquid evening':

The Pope and I, . . . solved the problem
Of his recalcitrant cashflow, at least temporarily.

We realise that this is a cul-de-sac or a counterfeit trail.
We won't find the real Judas here. Part Six, Nathanael or
Bartholomew being the Israelite without the guile, is
probably a more promising mineshaft, where we try to hear
his echo in 'you': 'You'll meet me in a twist in yourself . . .
meeting me in yourself, soon; but not yet' (168). For 'The
chosen few in the heavenly know' of part five the search is
both futile and unwarranted: (140)

> . . . I wish you, Judas, whatever is good
> For you, you are strange to me as loved, lost God.
> You were of us, in us, one, though now I hear you
>   are bad,
> Bad lad, bad lad, bad lad, bad lad.

After all, as the title of that poem tells us: 'Strangers are
strangers'. For the rest of us who continue the search
through the eighth part, where doubting Thomas could be
guide, we find as we go down into 'the dark night of the
hole' that, in fact, it's 'all the same in the dark': (201)

> . . . I have this vision of the world as a man
> With mean eyes and a hideous jollity in his voice
> I smell his heart, his guts, I absorb his rot.
>
> In spite of that, on certain days I see
> This odius contraption is preferable to me.

We discover that 'He was a pure disruptive music/ Alive
in me when I was with him' (213) and that 'He vanished out
of himself and became/ The music living in me, I listened to
him/ In myself till I knew I could say me . . . I am the music
now. Play me.' (214) And so we reach the point of
'Spiritfuck' where: (221)

> I sat alone and knew I had to open
> Myself as I had never opened before.
> I must be more open than any wound
> Or any door
> Anywhere.

We know that even the dark or darkness is not the answer because, in reality, we discover it to be 'The Green Dark' – a selfindulgently Irish form of darkness (225):

I know, in the green dark, I have not solved myself . . .

. . . I am all, and none of these; and they are me.
The green dark is what you dream it to be.

And so we reach the ninth stop: "I know I've arrived, can you tell me why I'm here?" *Here* 'I know in my heart I never perfected anything' (249) and 'I'm all flaws dreaming of some flawless thing':

> Even now, out of the sexual dark
> I could rise
> And cut through the blindness
> Of my eyes

but 'something has exhausted me, I am trying to grasp something piteous beyond me, a search for some kind of writing, I misunderstand it all despite the evidence (247). *Here* the experience is: (252-3)

> To be stripped to the bone
> Beyond the bone
> To have even the memory of things
> Whipped into the never-happened no-part of the mind
> To know the final darkness is light
> Compared with the darkness beyond darkness.

Eventually this dark night of the soul brings us from the first 'do it' to the moment when 'It is done' (273) and we realize that seeking to betray the betrayer into words is a contradiction: 'Betrayed?. . . I betrayed nothing or what has become nothing worth betraying . . . I betrayed another kind of mind, a tolerant emptiness.' Thus, the voice and/or the person of Judas in the poem called 'Arrived' (281) become 'my age, my love, my self, my art.' There are levels and stages through which we have journeyed in darkness through Judas as personification of the age in which we live; as the Christian name for 'love'; as the secret of myself and, finally, as the betrayal which is art, the ultimate artifice.

Part Ten surveys possible character studies for the role of Judas in 'Some Lads': Beckett (285), Joyce (286), Pontius Pilate, 'a game lad', who 'did his Ph.D. on the theme of crucifixion in the Post-Post-Modern Novel'(289), Adam, Barrabas, Hitler, Herod and 'an epileptic fish-and-chip shitkicker from Tralee', the 'patron saint of rubbish dumps/ especially when rubbish dumps are people' (321). At the end of this chapter, 'the lads and I', that is to say, Captain Flanagan, Cardinal Caiaphas, Mr. Barrabas, Mr. Hitler and 'I, Judas Iscariot', take over 'personal control of the first person singular' and 'the authorship of this Book/ from my collaborator, Brendan Kennelly, who is a sick man'(323). However, with the help of none other than Michael Collins, the coup is foiled and the poet can lead us to the second last stage of the journey. Not, however, before we have second commercial break.

"He will be mist" is a pun on the aftermath of any disappearance and the betrayal of every cause by the followers who take over and fake fidelity to the founder. They will miss him as transparently as he will dissolve into mist. This is the post resurrection Judasmob, 'a plague of smile smile smile' as 'Sincere' as 'Sin Seer'. These are responsible for 'Herod's hiring' for 'The Situation' and for Christy Hannity (Christianity as pronounced in Ireland), the great betrayer himself and 'the most accomplished castrator of God's creatures in our pious island', defined as: 'Pretend to be what they believe you are/ You are what they believe they think' (333). And here we are at last at the end of the penultimate book, which might even have been that second commercial break itself, 'A modest advertising campaign' (337). We reach 'The Line' (336) before the last and twelfth chapter called "The True Thing"(339). This 'straight black absolute line' is the one we have to cross to get to 'the true thing'. 'The line is there between us to keep us together'(336) it is also 'down the middle of my head' but the important thing is to 'get it, read it' (342) as the poet tells us, 'There's no escape'.

A poem called 'The Present Writer' (353) describes, in humorous fashion, the kind of humility required to undertake this labour. 'His face was unctioned in the muck' and 'his fingers flicked like rats among the filth'. You cannot clean the Augean stables without getting shit on your hands, nor can you understand what you are doing without baptism by muck, only the excremental evangelist, 'the stinking get', can 'tell my story'.

At this final stage of the journey, under the auspices of the twelfth apostle, Judas himself, Kennelly realises that the Judasvoice is possibly the voice of poetry itself which is 'betraying the promise, the beginning'. He admits in the preface(12):

> This last section shocked me. Everybody knows that the literary world . . . can be hate-riddled . . . I've heard people say, 'Poets are self-centered, malignant bastards, aren't they, really?' . . . The implication is that poetry is produced *in spite of* the nature of these . . . souls. *The Book of Judas* explores the possibilty that 'beauty' is produced because of it. Judas has a permanent residence on the human tongue.

Poetry is language as a betrayer of secrets. It is a 'freedom' created by and through 'unbridled, passionate muttering'; the thin line between silence and speech, truth and treachery(357):

> I understand the terror on the face of silence
> Confronted with my clichés.
> From the timber and steel of words I try to
> Construct a few bridges . . .
>
> Is there a language on earth my use of it won't betray?
> No wonder the silence is afraid of me.

The silence can only be betrayed into words by a slip of the Judastongue. Nothing can only become something by betrayal of itself. Out of the 'unbridled, passionate muttering' of poetry suddenly 'revelations' come:

> It is true I fail at the level of language
> When I try to translate the various parts
> Of myself into words to be read by others
> Interested in verbal revelations of the heart.

In the second part of this poem called 'Revelations' (356) we find the image which betrays the meaning: 'Consider my brain ticking like a nailbomb in a bag outside a supermarket. . . Who'll be passing when the nailbomb kicks?' The image is the poetic language which carries the revelation beyond the dumb silence of words. It is a bomb placed in the shadows, which, when it explodes will light up the darkness.

This image of a bomb is used throughout the *Book of Judas* to describe variously, Jesus, God, love, poetry and Judas himself. As we reach the last pages of the poem we realise that the poet has been guilty of the ultimate treachery, which is that the book itself is a carefully devised 'time bomb' that, when discovered, will 'chutzpah his poem' (359). It is treachery then because we understand in that final explosion that *The Book of Judas* is, in fact, about God and not, as we had been given to believe, about his opposite, the dog, Judas. It is a 'gospel' or 'godspell', which betrayed us, yet again, with a kiss. All the humour and scatology of the four hundred pages are bits of flesh scattered to distract the watchdogs, eloquent screams to satisfy the torturers who are trying to force the poet to betray his silence. The long scatalogue of hitmen, or shitmen, are mercenaries hired to do the entertaining dirtywork and keep the real protagonist's name clean. Kennelly, who has already been through the hands of Cromwell is a spy worthy of the name. In Judas he is disguised as James Bomb, double agent 012. Just as the real thing ended in suicide, so does the poem. It explodes in our faces. The final word is 'bomb', 'going boom, coming boom bloody boom boy boom' (107). The bomb has been carefully and strategically laid throughout the poem 'in the timid corners of time' (58), 'in the box in the corner of the living-room' (107). It has appeared as God in 'God is a bomb' (119), as love and as poetry 'when a man explodes, be it in poetry or love' (302) and as Christ, 'a bomb of a man'(58). It ends up personifying Judas so that we can hardly tell one from the other. In the 'Final Letter' (304) we 'realise that in the end (and the letter is from the Bomb himself) will be The Word and The Word is me.' The poem has led the poet to the tricky revelation that the bomb is the nature of Judas and one that he shares with God in all three persons, with love and with poetry. The poem has detected the bomb, is a bomb detector as well as a bomb in itself:

> Bombs have a tricky habit of betraying
> The intentions of the bomber. (109)

And so the poet standing at the end of the line, his own hangman, bomb in hand, admits that:

> Being your own hangman demands
> A poetic sense of timing
> In that final stanza you discover
> Sweet secrets of rhythm and rhyming.

The last word, that recapitulating image of the poem is 'bomb': Judas is a bomb, God is a bomb, love is a bomb and this poem is a bomb. What could that possibly mean?

Essentially it means that what Judas does for Jesus, what love does for time, what time does for God, what God does for word, what word does for language, are one and the same thing: blowing them 'out of their tiny mind' into a new kind of existence. 'I began my correspondence with the Bomb' the poet tells us, using correspondence as a pun meaning 'letters' and 'similarity': (302)

> Because I sensed we were two of a kind.
> 'Dear Bomb' I wrote in my opening letter

'Did you ever feel you were going out of your mind?'

and The Bomb replies in words which again apply to all the synonyms: 'I'd feel better if I could do what I am best at. Explode.' The being of God, of Christ, of humanity, of time and of prose is 'at its best' when exploded. Poetry is language erupting like a volcano, flowing like lava (17) and (119):

> God is a bomb
> To get the best results, handle carefully,
> Time properly, chose a fruitful place,
> Where you can turn murder into martyrdom.
>
> Follow these instructions or it's likely
> Godbomb will blow up in your face.
> Who'll clean up the mess then. Bloody disgrace!

Bloody dis-grace is Judas. He was essential to Christ's resurrection, the bombing at rushhour when time stood still. All the other disciples were 'men and women with appropriate names, disposable' (130). Only Judas was 'necessary'; together they form 'an unlimited company' (227) and 'the bond between that man and me will go on and on' (109). Every other bond is expendable, 'but who can replace that other ? or me ?' (130)

A similar relationship exists between poetry and prose: 'Semtex is more powerful than disruptive prose' (121):

> If you're compelled to polite your way through lies
> And live the death of the average non-man
> Semtex is the line for you,
> The only line your heart will know is true.

'When a man explodes, be it in poetry or love' (302) or resurrection, he begins to exist. Most of us prefer non-existence (242):

. . .Whatever love is
It's what I fly from
My heart will never house an unexploded bomb.

If you keep yourself open to the other, the possible, the Judaskiss which will betray your cosy secluded garden, then you will be ready for 'your very own bomb on its missionary way' (201). The explosive quality of words is recognized by 'Ozzie' in his inimitable way: (38)

Words are to kummynikate sez I
like shit sez ozzie won good bomm
blow de whole fukken world ta hell

The same is also true for God: 'A moment of love' for him is also 'the way he explodes ' (58) into existence. The resurrectional pattern of the bomb transfigures being into existence, sameness into otherness, 'In there' into 'Out there' (284):

Out there in there

Bomb is tired squatting there, doing nothing,
Just waiting for that ultimate ecstasy.
This morning, Bomb said it was planning
To play with modern poetry.

'Out there in there where the last word won't go
Where no word has ever been
I would like to hear a poem ticking
Like my heart. Let the Tick
Be tender blunt uncouth obscene

I will study it more mercilessly than anyone
Has studied me. Tick, tick, I will make
That tick my own,
Plant it in a word I will menace into being,
A word to do with known, unknown,
In me of me beyond me
Breeding a new ancient poem

Tick, tick,
I will study
Until it merges with my bone,
Bonepoem, bombpoem,
One-word-poem-tick-tick-way-of-seeing
Into the flash that is beyond all believing'.

This poem summarizes the apocalyptic energy of the bomb as the essence of all that is, all that seeks release from its own being-there, all that 'is tired squatting there'. We all await 'that ultimate ecstasy' which is the transformation of 'out there' (Being/God) or 'In there' (existence/Humanity) into its opposite, achieved by menacing it 'into being' through a word that is 'beyond me' and which explodes the 'me' in 'the flash that is beyond all believing'. This 'menace', this 'bomb' can be called Judas, who has been since the beginning of time, 'before his ancestors arrived on the scene, he was.' After the unborn will have ceased to exist, he'll be . . . Time is merely a stage where his reticent yet theatrical spirit is repeated and refined'(12).

I've no time for that reincarnation stuff
And yet I know a truth I cannot prove.
I was a bomb in another life. (269)

Judas is the principle in the Godhead which first betrayed itself into existence, into incarnation, the word made flesh at the beginning of time. This poem has led us through the poet to the realisation of Judascape.

This word is also a double agent, revealing as much as it betrays of the reality it seeks to circumscribe. It combines 'inscape' and 'escape' in its definition of Judas. Kennelly's poem shows that the myth of the double-crossing Judas is a 'crossword' (157) of the 'shake, shade, shape or shame' of nothing. 'Nothing pretending to be all'. In the poem 'A voice at last' the poet 'suddenly decided to be the first spokesman for nothing' (354).

Nothing, I studied it in my breast, in yours,
In all the victims I have mentioned elsewhere,
I spoke out, nobody listened, everyone
Thought he was something, I persisted,
Slowly, the scene changed, my best endeavours
Tell me that nothing is coming into its own,
Nothing has a voice at last. Listen! Listen!

Poetry as the voice of 'nothing' is the snake that slithers between us and the blight of bliss, opening the possiblity of exile and freedom, our very 'Judasout into the desert' (304). It is the hissing sound that betrays; the Judaskiss that delivers us from Jesusfreakery; the muttering *non serviam* that initiated freedom. Judas is the fourth person of the Trinity who has been nothing since the beginning of time, and since nothing is the opposite of God, the escape route which betrayed the godhead into the otherness, which is incarnation. So, in reality nothing matters like hell and 'at the heart of nothingmatters, love is born' (58). It is through the machinations of Judas, The Bomb, that all existence is realized. Judas is nothing other than the space between God and mankind, the 'dividing line' (336), the 'Zone' (109) or nomansland, saving each from the absorption in the other. Judas is his 'own little holy land' where a sound can go forth which rearranges the metrics, rhythms and music of either partner, the word or line 'dividing me from my redeemer' but also creating the betrayal into error where 'a perfect form is shaped through fault' (58). Judas is that double agent, that counter-intelligence saboteur and subversive snake in the grass, whose 'unbridled passionate muttering' changed history into poetry, predictable parallel lines into electrifying crosswords, whose Janus-like, grade-crossing bifidity has surreptitiously saved us from God and God from us.

GABRIEL FITZMAURICE: ARTIST AND CULTURAL ENTREPRENEUR
BY GERARD QUINN

Gabriel Fitzmaurice loves his family, his parish, his half-county, county, province and country strictly in that order. He is a rooted man who cares for things close to him and far from him in that order. So he must be introduced as of this townland and of that family.

He was born in December 1952 in Moyvane, Co. Kerry, only child of Jack and Maud (Cunningham) Fitzmaurice, both of whom were from families that had farmed in Moyvane for generations. Gabriel's interest in the arts came mainly from his mother who was very interested in literature and music. Apart from fluent Irish and French, Maud would humorously insist that she had two English languages, one "standard" and one the local dialect. She and her husband Jack ran a shop in Moyvane until early heart trouble ruled out physical work, after which early failure of eyesight ruled out reading. But she was still undaunted: she kept her mind fresh by using books-on-tape and listening to the radio. Gabriel can remember literary discussion between his mother and the local teachers, at other times with the PP Edmond Fitzpatrick, or with John Moriarty, variously described as local genius, mystic, philospher, National Teacher turned University lecturer turned gardener – now living in Connemara. Maud Fitzmaurice took care to pass on to her son her interest in good literature as he grew up, countering the instant pleasure and ideological brainwashing of *Dandy*, *Beano*, *Hornet* and *Hotspur*. In spite of her handicaps Maud lived fully until her death in 1974. Of great support to her was the appreciation and love of her husband Jack, a "very steady man" who ran the shop until he retired some years ago.

Jack's people were great set-dancers. His ancestral home in Glenalappa continued the céili-house tradition of house-dances which would help account for the sociability of Fitzmaurice Senior, as would his having 13 brothers and sisters with a reputation as great drinkers. When the Fitzmaurice family, aunts, uncles, and cousins, reunited (or most of it) in Glenalappa, they hit Moyvane seven nights a week ("Christ, the hangovers!"), and when the word went out that they were approaching Dinny Mack's pub, musicians materialised and there were set dances.

Ní nach ionadh, it was this musical strand that Gabriel developed first. In his initial teaching post in Avoca, Co. Wicklow he formed a rock band which became the regular relief band in the Centre in Arklow. They wrote their own songs which exercised the talent for writing which he had kept hidden in Secondary School, and almost hidden in Mary Immaculate College of Education. But in Wicklow it was soon a choice between teaching and music. He opted to stay teaching, and returned to the school in Moyvane in 1975, just in time to teach in the old 1888 school and help carry a strand of tradition into the new buildings in September. Tradition is important to him: as he says, "We cannot live in the past. But the past can live in us."

Being young and enthusiastic he joined everything in the parish, the GAA club (selector for the football team that won the North Kerry League in 1977); Secretary of the Development Association for a while. He was also secretary of the local Housing Committee and a member of the Parish Committee.

From 1975 till 1979 Fitzmaurice acted with the Listowel Drama Group, playing Algernon in *The Importance of Being Earnest*; Shawn Keogh in *The Playboy*; George in Thornton Wilder's *Our Town*; and, like all great actors, he played Buttons in *Cinderella*!

In Moyvane and their neighbouring parishes he met traditional musicians and learned their music, which he found expressed him better than rock did. So he became chairman of Knockanure Comhaltas Ceoltóirí Éireann for a number of years, during which he played a lot of music in North Kerry and West Limerick, from Listowel to Newcastlewest: Moyvane, Knockanure, Athea, Abbeyfeale, Glin, Carrickerry, Ardagh, Tarbert.

While collecting local songs in 1975, Gabriel Fitzmaurice met a man called Con Greaney, and what followed is a fine example of unselfish talent-spotting which found an artist aged 63, for whom he won wide recognition, as well as bringing delight to the thousands of people who would enjoy his art. Now 82, Con is peaking in his career.

Gabriel took Con to the studio for the tape *Between the Hills and Sea* in Spring 1991, and afterwards persuaded Oidhreacht to provide funds for him to bring out a solo tape of Con's – it came out in October 1991 [Pat's Tracks OIDH 002]. Con has since recorded another tape entitled *The Road to Athea,* Cló Iar-Chonnachta (CIC 082). Gabriel regards Con as an example of how to live life in a small rural area – he has guessed Con's philosophy is a) be yourself, b) express your talents, c) stand by three f's – Friendship, Fun and Freedom, d) don't worry. Gabriel has absorbed some of this philosophy and found it useful in shaping his own life. He found another older man, Martin Mulvihill, the celebrated fiddler, a bit like that too, and related well to him. As an only child Fitzmaurice feels he relates best to older people and to children.

When he arrived home from Wicklow in 1975, Listowel Writers' Week had been running for four years, and through meeting poets and painters etc. etc. so near home, he soon became interested in writing. Michael Hartnett was living nearby in Templeglantine, and about 1979 he and Gabriel became very friendly – meeting for a few jars on a Saturday when they would discuss poetry, *Gaeilge*, translation etc. etc. In the same year Fitzmaurice joined Writers' Week as director of its ballad competition, "for a newly composed ballad."

I think this first engagement is significant. The ballad is an older and a folk genre, it is traditional. So why, we might ask, should there be a "newly composed" ballad? It would seem that an ongoing tradition of newly composed ballads would function as an absorption of new incidents into the traditional culture. Ballads are a part of the process by which the values of a culture are communicated. And new ballads use the old rhythms to assimilate the most disparate experience, and mediate it for the locality. At a macro-level a national language facilitates this: each country filters new ideas through its language, so as to absorb what suits its nature and reject what would cause too great a culture-shock. But when Ireland lost its language it lost this filter, and now its ozone layer is very thin. A person who tackles what Gabriel Fitzmaurice has done is confronting one of the great cultual problems of the twentieth century. Or as Shakespeare's Irishman put it, "What ish my nation?" How do you hold onto a national identity in the hurricane of communications? What happens local traditions, what happens national traditions? Is the filter of Irish language needed to ensure continuity, or will some form of Anglo-Irish speech stand in for the same work? Or is Anglo-Irish speech a fading trace of Gaelic speech in our increasingly standard English? Did Joyce's *Ulysses* answer the question, or did it make some aspects of the question irrelevant? Some Irish poets say the question is irrelevant, but do they say this because they have not got Irish? Michael Hartnett knows Irish and has tackled the question with energy, saying farewell to English more than once. One can feel the pain of his concern, and admire the art in which he expresses it. Gabriel Fitzmaurice is also a fluent Irish speaker and is trying to cope with the problem; and he does it in his inimitable way by refusing to be daunted, refusing to agonise, thinking positively, insisting on making small actual gains for his locality. He would insist that the great social bonding that happens at football matches and sessions of song must continue and the new names and deeds must be absorbed by new ballads. There is a poem in Fitzmaurice's forthcoming book *The Village Sings* in which he tackles this idea, one that is central to the life-undertaking he has set himself. Dedicated to the memory of his mother's brother Billy Cunningham who farmed in Moyvane and was a great singer of ballads, the poem is called *Hence the Songs* –

How soon great deeds are abstract . . .

Hence the songs –
The mighty deeds the tribe sings in the bar:
Gaisce diminished by the video.

Men I never knew still star
In North Kerry Finals,
Their deeds not history but myth
Alive upon a singer's breath;

Again local men are martyred
In a lonely glen;

Now love is lost,
A Rose is won –

Things insufficient till they're sung.

The intrusive video, whose slick professionalism can hide the irrelevance of its offerings, should not be allowed to diminish our local, personal and loving things, our memories and hopes, our self-respect, our identity. ("Turn off that bloody transistor, Billy's going to give us a song.")

From his significant beginning as director of the newly composed ballad competition, he went on to become programme director and eventually chairman (1982-1985, & 1991-1992). During this time he brought the well known John McGahern, Eavan Boland, Nuala Ní Dhomhnaill, John Montague, D.J. Enright and many others to Listowel. He brought Professor Augustine Martin, Professor Johnny Coolahan, Declan Kiberd, Fintan O'Toole to lecture in Listowel. And in the 21st birthday year he brought President Mary Robinson to open Writers' Week.

But he also achieved the scoops that every director and chairman wishes for. He brought Kazuo Ishiguro before he won the Booker Prize, Ted Hughes before he was made Laureate, and Roddy Doyle before he was well known. This spotting of talent before it is universally recognized is important cultural work for the nation, but equally is of huge value to North Kerry in bringing them a sophisticated self-esteem. North Kerry has even been given a European dimension through Gabriel Fitzmaurice's last major contribution to Writers' Week – he brought over the poets Liliana Ursu (Romania) and Gyözö Ferencz (Hungary) whom he had met at the European Poetry Festival in Louvain.

He has for the moment retired from the hugely time-consuming front line in the Writers' Week team, but occasionally lends a hand when called upon.

The Poetry

In 1984, Fitzmaurice published a remarkable first book of poetry called *Rainsong* which was well received by the critics. Writing about it, Brendan Kennelly spoke of the young poet's easy skill and his variety of styles. He noted that Fitzmaurice already had his own voice, a musical, intelligent and honest voice, and that he was confident and sensitive. I remember one of the poems in that collection very clearly. It showed local people being cold to a man who had lost the power to be sociable. The man had started off well:

> A colossus on the playing field.
> A great man for the crack.

But then something went wrong –

> For years he spoke to no one
> But turned his sagging back on people,
> Head down, he would cycle into town.
>
> Whispers prodded that he be seen to
> "Looked after", slyly said.
> Anyone could see
> That his head was out of joint.
> And he couldn't even hold his lonely pint.
>
> They found him hanging in the barn: dead.

Some kindness now – a bit late:

Viciousness turned almost to understanding.
Living alone, never wed . . .
"His uncle did it years before him.
Kind for him," they said.

In one line of this poem there is a combination of the strands that make his best poetry. "And he couldn't even hold his lonely pint" is first of all the crude idiomatic taunt of a broken culture which has no criterion for measuring value but a person's pint-rating. Crossed on this crudity is the sensitivity of "lonely", so that the line achieves a delicate balance between rough and gentle. But there is more to the line. The "hold" and "lonely" speak to each other as in Gaelic poetry – so well brought to English by Clarke and Hartnett. And finally the line has the easy flow of ballad.

In this early poem you can already sense Fitzmaurice's tolerant mind – there is room in a healthy parish for different kinds of people. In fact there should be room inside each of us for two different people. "Am wolf", he said in one poem, and 3 lines later – as if influenced by Blake's *Innocence and Experience* – "Am lamb". If we know ourselves well, we know both sides of ourselves. One is an outlaw.

The first book had a wide range of theme and tone. Some poems were humorous. One poem for instance succeeded very well in talking about women and Guinness at the same time:

She was velvet, lily cream
And then I loved her
And love her yet
Through froth of hate.

Also in the first book was a fine poem called "Rain", full of rich crazy imagery. It presents a large woman with great physical and emotional needs. She was never satisfied until one day a man turned up who was as unusal as herself. He was damaged like an oak that was hit by lightning, and maybe because of that, they got on very well. The poem – "Rain" – is a successful blend of earthiness and magic. Of

136

his first book Conor Kelly wrote that it contained "the sense of poetry as an art, a craft and a vocation in words . . . *Rainsong* marks the debut of an original talent." John F. Deane called the book "well-ordered, well thought out [with a] strong sense of ballad-rhythms . . . The poems are offered as lived experiences carefully thought over. That gives them a wisdom, and a searching quality."

There is often a sort of impish delight in Gabriel's work, not unlike the quality to be found in *The Magic Glasses* by George Fitzmaurice. But as well as the devilment there is always a largeness of vision, magnanimity; there is no pettiness anywhere in his poetry. He is a complete Christian. However, he is just as complete a pagan, and refuses to be *claonta* in the matter: it is refreshing.

He had a second book in 1987, called *Road to the Horizon*, the centrepiece in which was a long poem called *The Hurt Bird*. This was a simple poem. And deep. It brings you right back to when you were eight or nine years old. There is a classroom of children who have been allowed to the window to look at birds on the ice in the playground. They are indentifying rooks, and jackdaws – "the black birds. Blackbirds? (Laughter)": little touches like that one show how razor-sharp is teacher Fitzmaurice's grasp of a child's mind. But the poem also shows how subtle is his sense of the relationship between reality and language, between things and their names. e.g. You are walking along a country road and suddenly you notice – maybe a wild flower – you are astonished at the reality and you really look at it for a moment. You have suddenly seen the reality. And your defences all come down. And then you shake yourself and turn to someone and say: "Now what is that called?"

Or another e.g. it is a person you think you know all about, and suddenly you see through to a new area you never thought existed: there is a quantum-jump in your relationship with that person. Children have experiences like this more than us with our habit behaviour. So these hurt-bird moments are very precious. They are mystical – seeing some aspect of reality for the first time. And Gabriel Fitzmaurice's poem *The Hurt Bird* celebrates an extended sequence of such moments in a classroom, where a good teacher understands what is happening in the children's minds and handles the situation with great mastery. Only at the end of the lesson do the children begin to look for names for the astonishing reality they have experienced.

Another aspect of Fitzmaurice's poetry, to be seen in *The Hurt Bird* is the absence of any trace of "Look how clever I am" that some poets use. There is a natural authentic quality about his poetry. And this also applies to the rhythms he uses. As with the "lonely pint", all the rhythms, even his free verse or ballads, have an instinctual flow.

He has the poet's love of a good word. In the poem "Rain" one line goes: "Prayer was wagtails in the morning." – the unusual couple are praying. Wag/tail. You can hear the resilience in the middle of the word. Word-music. And you will find items like "A tracery of swallow/Streaks the grass."

His third book *Dancing Through* (1990) has what many books of poetry lack – it has several poems that the reader remembers and goes back to read again. And there are memorable images in other poems, such as that for the fiddle-playing of Martin Mulvihill: "silence softly singing/Through the wood and steel". Much pain is brought to book in this collection, but not always is it raised clearly to the level of art as it is in "Predator", a poem about the alien harshness of a crowd of rooks experienced when a person goes into the woods alone: "As if the crows could turn away the stranger, / They wheel their frantic chainsaw-song of fright." – an excellent mimesis of mechanical rejection.

In the poem "Winter", dedicated to his friends Pádraig and Rosemarie Hogan, plants and ideas are left to an istinctual hibernation in a gentle sensuous place:

> my beds are planted
> my roses pruned
> my borders coddled in turf-dust . . .
>
> The gardener has tended all he must

And in the poem that follows, "The Pregnant Earth," after speaking about personal hurt and darkness, he develops the idea presented in *Winter*. He combines sexuality with the maturity of a poetic idea inside the womb of the mind in a celebration of the therapeutic value of art. The poem ends with some of the finest lines Fitzmaurice has written:

> The pregnant earth,
> Midwinter,
> Sings its song to me;
> Humming in its belly:
> *Arise, Persephone* ...
>
> This simple song sustains me
> As the darkness claims its dead –
>
> O light within the darkness:
> O carol in my head ...

– where the midwinter word "carol" brings the reverence, newbirth and promise of salvation of Christmas, adding to it the hint of woman's name, and is also a lyrical name for a poem.

A woman's help again was instrumental in moving him lightly from pain to happiness in *An Gáire*, a particularly good poem in the collection *as Gaeilge* called *Nocht*, published by Coiscéim in 1989, in which we are given six steps of a rake's progress of which the fifth is:

> Gháir me leis an meisce:
> Moladh le seachrán –
> Is d'fhreagair na gloiní folmha:
> A amadáin, a amadáin ... [1]

---

[1] I cried out to drunken-ness!
O, to be astray –
And the emptied glasses answered:
You fool, you fool ...

"Dánta dea-mhúnlaithe" was Liam Prút's comment on the book: "Well made poems".

Another poem from *Dancing Through* might be approached by way of *Cat* in *Nocht* – cats and children being good at sizing up people. Fitzmaurice describes the cat's movements around a house, and how slow she is to accept advances made by strangers:

> "Tomhaiseann sí bronntóir/Sara nglacann sí bia."
> [She sizes up the giver/Before she accepts the food.]

This same carefulness is found in a new pupil in Gabriel's poem called *Getting to Know You*. In this poem, the boy is testing the master to see if he was worth giving loyalty to . The new boy is called Thomas:

> Thomas,
> You don't trust me –
> I can tell from your trapped eyes.
> How can I help you,
> My sulky friend?
> Tell you I love you?
> (That would seem like lies)
> To reach out to touch you
> Might offend . . .
>
> Coax you with tacit kindness:
> Greet you, man to man . . .
>
> Yes, Thomas,
> I am strong
> (But equal) –
> And, Thomas,
> We are both 'at school':
> Both circling round
> A common understanding:
> Both sniffing at the smile
> That sweetens rules.

Today you bounce up to me,
Your eyes the rising sun:

We share your secret story –

Hello!
God bless you,
Tom . . .

That is of course about becoming acquainted with a new
person, but like a lot of Fitzmaurice's other poems it is also
about authenticity in any relationship, and quite specially in a
teacher- pupil relationship. And finally it is about a basic
democratic equality between himself and all creation.

As for the pagan strand in Gabriel, he has left us a
description of a wild physical source of his poetic thinking.
His donkey in *The Wild Ass* is

King of moor and bogland
One with lark and frog,
Who sensed firm from treacherous
In the scarred bog

This donkey is "The metaphor, the Christopher," the
carrier of Christ indeed, but Fitzmaurice's sensibility is not
dissociated. In his metaphors, the sensitive Christ element
coexists with the physical and sensuous. The next line, last
line, of this poem sums it up, "You fart within my mind."

The last poem I would like to consider from *Dancing
Through* is "Communion" in which again the ballad's
importance is presented in context of the pub's importance
for social and cultural continuity and refreshment. A woman
sings and wins the acclaim of silence amidst pub-talk. The
poem has strength, and sensuous physicality, and
gentleness:

And the loud men fell to silence.

They belong to the singing girl,
Her voice as clear
As birdsong before rain.
The song is in their bellies now,
And beer burps along
And thumbs its nose at pain.

In a review of *Dancing Through*, Sean Dunne put his
finger on a factor which occasionally mars some of
Fitzmaurice's poems (and the comment applies also to some
poems in *The Road to the Horizon*): "Now and then, he's
inclined to stray towards the abstract and towards capital
letters in ways that perhaps lessen the effect of what he has
to say." But, equally, Dunne has praise which also applies
to the fine poems in all three books which touch on incidents
in the lives of commonfolk: "His turn of mind is naturally
reflective and celebratory and when this meets the hard and
detailed grit of everyday life, his work is at its most
rewarding."

Gabriel Fitzmaurice's most recent book *The Father's
Part* is a celebration of his adopted, his thoroughly adopted,
son John. We would of course agree with the publisher that
it is "A must book for anyone interested in Family, and
adopted families, especially." But there are universal items
in it. The tenderness of *Bedtime* about the child who refuses
to go to sleep, but cannot be commanded by words.

Defeated,
I take you to my bed
And lie beside you.

You tug my hair,
Gouge my eyes,
Babble,
Kick.

If you had words
You wouldn't be so spoiled –

Unbroken
On the bit of language
Yet, sweet child.

There is also the moving poem *Presentation* of the acceptance of the child, adopted child, by Tom, in the ancestral home:

This is the floor
Tom's father crawled,
My father crawled.

Mary,
Woman of the house,
Coaxes him across the floor.

Now
You're a Fitzmaurice.

Any charge of hubris in this situation is answered by the fact that it is not sheer tribalism: it is softened by the delicate fact that the parents are vulnerable. They have risked going outside themselves to make this child flesh of their flesh and this is a key moment in the bonding. In this book there are other good things, but readers should not miss *Holy Thursday*, *Approaching Pentecost*, and *Your Name*.

Just now, Fitzmaurice has a number of poems towards a further volume to be called *The Village Sings* which will include some political poems. The poem I have highest regard for in this new collection as it stands so far is *The Lone Star Trail*:

It started as a song –
A simple round
Of cowboys and of cattle

Till sound possessed the children
Who yelled

And neighed
And mooed:

Cowboy was a horse
And both were cattle.

Then the song became their pictures
Swift and rude.

They offer me their pictures for approval
(All suns and no horizons) . . .

I approve.

Here for a a short interval children are free from the
world of logic (where law and business rule). In this lesson
in music, drama and choreography, a lesson too in seeing
both sides of a story, followed by a lesson in art, the
children live in the world created by their imaginations,
where no boundaries divide up the many roles, empathising
with everything. As in the case of *The Hurt Bird*, pupils are
fortunate to be in such a classroom where their teacher
shows a clear understanding of their world, a world where
each person is an intense central sun, and where no one
wants the boundary-limits of a horizon.

There is a selection from all the Fitzmaurice poems
available on tape from Cló Iar-Chonnachta, Indreabhán,
Conamara (L14, 1992).

Gabriel Fitzmaurice has turned his hand to a number of
things calculated to improve the quality of life in North
Kerry. He, along with co-producers Pat Donegan and
Richard Casey, has provided an opportunity for people in
Kerry and elsewhere to hear eleven of their own local
singers singing the songs and ballads of Kerry with true
indigenous interpretation and rhythms. The tape *Between
the Hills and Sea* was produced at Pat's Tracks [OIDH 001]
Recording Studio, Causeway, Co. Kerry. One of the singers
on this tape was Con Greaney who has since featured with
his talent-scout on RTE's *The Pure Drop*.

A welcome book of verses for the young, *The Moving Stair,* was published by The Kerryman in 1989. The verses in this book are in touch with the experiences of youngsters, for example those whose younger sisters and brothers scribble on their copies (it's their world, and we never fail to get a shock when we empathise with a child and see how actually huge some apparently small thing is). For a young person it is a consolation to find that the disruption of the arrival of a new brother or sister has been felt by others. And it is therapeutic to find ways of laughing in the classroom at what caused horror when it happened, as in the case of getting lost in town.

> Once when I was shopping
> With Daddy in Tralee
> I got lost in this hardware shop.
> I looked but couldn't see . . .

We are of course not dealing with art, but we are dealing with other no less important aspects of a culture. And a book like this is an excellent teaching tool helping the child to see how many ways there are of handling experience, in this case laughing at former pain. (Poolbeg have reprinted an enlarged edition of this book.)

A more heavyweight project than these children's books and tapes of songs was *An Crann Faoi Bhláth*, an anthology of modern poetry *as Gaeilge* with translations, which Gabriel Fitzmaurice collaborated with Declan Kiberd to produce for Wolfhound in 1991. Included in the anthology is an excerpt from Fitzmaurice's own fine translation of *An Phurgóid* by Mícheál Ó hAirtnéide, a translation which catches the wit, devilment and pain of the original text. Sean Dunne called it "vigorous and hectic"; no reader can fault Dunne's high praise. "It has a great energy about it and gets across the images of the original with a brio that makes it stand as a poem in its own right."

Sea, tagann an tinfeadh, ach níl mé sásta –
Clagairt poigheachán seilide atá fágtha
Is carn crotail ciaróg marbh é,
an dán millte le baothráiteas
tá ag sú na fola as ealaín ársa
mar sciortán ar mhagairle madra.

which is well caught in:

Inspiration comes, and the poet is left
with the empty rattle of discarded shells,
the husks of beetles piled up dead –
his poem spoiled by stupid talk
that sucks the blood of an ancient craft
like a bloated tick on a mongrel's balls.

Mícheál Ó hAirtnéide has probably forgiven the
reviewer in *The Irish Times* for mistakenly thinking that
Ó hAirtnéide himself and not Gabriel Fitzmaurice had made
the translations, and, worse, for compounding the error by
finding the translations had "a stylistic assurance and lyric
flow which is far more developed than in the originals."
This is nonsense, but the translations are very good:
Ó hAirtnéide would have known that the English of Gabriel
Fitzmaurice would be free of "*gaoth is glicbhéarla.*"[1]

In the case of translating Seán Ó Ríordáin, Fitzmaurice
must have had much problem-solving, because the poems
are modernist, so that difficulty, irony and paradox is of the
essence. Yet his translation keeps not only Ó Ríordáin's
complex ideas but his rhythms and word-play. The poem
Saoirse for instance is all of it a fascinating read – we have
room for only three lines:

Is ceanglód an chonairt smaointe
Tá ag drannadh im thimpeall
San uaigneas:

---

[1] * (lit) "wind and cheap English"

well rendered by :

And I will tie the thought-pack, wheeling
and snarling all around me
in my solitude:

His translation of "Inis Córthaidh Agus Gné Den Stair"
by Art Ó Maolfabhail is also particularly successful. In this
anthology we find Gabriel Fitzmaurice giving his energy to
activity that strengthens the culture not just of Kerry but of
the whole country. The book has been hailed as "the best-
edited and most critically authoritative anthology of
contemporary poetry in Irish, with or without translations."
    There is no man more humble and generous in
acknowledging help than Gabriel Fitzmaurice. He says he
learned an awful lot from Michael Hartnett. And he received
a lot of help from Brendan Kennelly – positive criticism,
introductions to various people etc. He adds that Declan
Kiberd's opinions are valued. But in his wife Brenda
(Downey) from Tarbert he has found an enormous
influence, not just as a friend/lover/wife and now mother;
but as an excellent literate/educated reader whose responses
are invaluable.
    Fitzmaurice is a scholar and a gentleman. He has also
the common touch. An he has the energy of a JCB.
Somewhere in Ireland there may be two or three who are his
equal as cultural entrepreneur and artist. If so, more power
to them. We can only wish that every district in Ireland had
people so well equipped and so unselfishly willing to
revitalise their area.
    His little poem *Dancing Through* compares footballer
Mikey Sheehy to Nureyev the Ballet Dancer, calling him
"flesh of tribal soul". It needed to be said that a county's
best footballers are an incarnation of the spirit of the county:
"O flesh of tribal soul". A Sheehy is not just playing for
Kerry, he is Kerry. The soul of Kerry has put on flesh. I
would go further and suggest that in the realm of the arts,
Gabriel Fitzmaurice himself, well-rooted man, son of Maud
and Jack, husband of Brenda, father of John and Nessa, has
already done a great deal to make flesh the tribal soul of

North Kerry. His work is enjoyed far from Kerry, but it is of deep relevance to his locality, and should be read by everyone there, for it is accessible, and consciously accessible. For he has said of himself that his "aim as a poet is to be a popular serious poet". Although still a young man, he has already done great work for the arts and education in Ireland. And perhaps the best thing he has done is to write a number of authentic poems that will stand the test of time.

Notes on the Contributors

PROFESSOR JOHN COOLAHAN is a native of Tarbert, Co. Kerry. He was educated at St. Ita's College, Tarbert, St. Patrick's College, Drumcondra, U.C.D. and T.C.D. He has a wide experience of teaching at all levels, and has lectured widely in Ireland and abroad. Among an extensive range of publications are his books, *Irish Education: Its History and Structure* and *The ASTI and Post-Primary Education in Ireland*. He has a keen interest in history, literature and drama. While head of a poetic theatre group in Dublin in the 'sixties he had close contact with Dr. MacGreevy, his fellow Tarbert man, who is the subject of his article. Dr. Coolahan has been Professor of Education in Maynooth College since 1987.

MARK PATRICK HEDERMAN is a Benedictine monk from Glenstal Abbey in Limerick. He was co-editor of *The Crane Bag Journal of Irish Studies* for nine years.

AUGUSTINE MARTIN MA, PH. D., was born in Ballinamore, Co. Leitrim and educated at Cistercian College, Roscrea and U.C.D. where he holds the chair of Anglo-Irish Literature and Drama. His books include a critical study of James Stephens, a biography of W.B. Yeats and a history of Anglo-Irish Literature. As editor he has published *Yeats' Collected Poems*, *Winter's Tales from Ireland*, *The Genius of Irish Prose*, *Forgiveness and Other Stories*, *James Joyce: The Artist and the Labyrinth*. He is currently engaged on the biography of Patrick Kavanagh.

A well-known broadcaster, he has devised and presented some thirty programmes for Telefis Scoile (Schools Television) and edited several series of Thomas Davis Lectures for Radio Éireann. He has been Visiting Professor to the universities of Hofstra and Miami (U.S.A.), of Waseda (Japan) and Caen (France). He was Chairman of the Abbey Board and Director of the Yeats International Summer School, Sligo. He is Founder and Director of the

James Joyce Annual Summer School, Newman House, U.C.D.

STEVE MATHESON is a career Civil Servant, working in London. A graduate of Aberdeen University, his interests include information technology, Scottish and Irish literature, the navy of Nelson's day, and cooking.
He is the author of *Maurice Walsh, Storyteller*, published by Brandon in 1985.
He is married, with two sons.

FINTAN O'TOOLE was born in Dublin in 1958. A former editor of *Magill* and former theatre critic of *In Dublin*, the *Irish Times* and the *Sunday Tribune*, he is at present a columnist with the *Irish Times*. He has been Literary Advisor to the Abbey Theatre. He is the author of three books, *The Politics of Magic: The Work and Times of Tom Murphy*, *No More Heroes: A Radical Guide to Shakespeare*, and *A Mass for Jessie James: A Journey through 1980's Ireland* as well as the pamphlet *The Southern Question*, all published by Raven Arts Press.

RICHARD PINE was co-editor of the *Irish Literary Supplement*. Author of books on international cultural policy, Oscar Wilde, the Dublin Gate Theatre and Lawrence Durell, his most recent publication is the highly acclaimed study *Brian Friel and Ireland's Drama*. He has edited a volume of essays on Brendan Kennelly – *Dark Fathers into Light*. He has lectured in cultural studies at many American and European universities and research institutes and broadcasts frequently on music and literature. He has served as Chairman of the Media Association of Ireland and as Secretary of the Irish Writers' Union, and is a consultant to the Council of Europe on cultural development programmes. He holds a public affairs appointment in Radio Telefis Éireann and is a Governor of the Royal Irish Academy of Music. He is currently completing a volume of essays on Ireland and the post-colonial world.

GERARD QUINN has lectured in English at Strawberry Hill College of Education, and at Carysfort College of Education, and is now a lecturer in English and American Literature at U.C.D.